Stewardship

By:

Dr. Gene Herndon

Printed in the United States of America

Published by Aion Multimedia
20118 N 67th Ave
Suite 300-446
Glendale AZ 85308
www.aionmultimedia.com

ISBN: 9780991565795

TABLE OF CONTENTS

SOWING
Transactional vs. Investment Mindset

Genesis 8:22

"While the earth remaineth, seedtime and harvest, and cold and heat, and summer and winter; day and night shall not cease."

Do we still have day and night? Do we still have summer and winter? Do we still have heat and cold? Of course we do. Lake Havasu is about 10 degrees hotter than Phoenix. I was there once in November at a meeting with my spiritual grandfather. At my hotel, they had a little plaque that said, "Today's weather is hot and sunny." So I asked the woman at the desk, "How many times does that thing get changed?" She said, "Really, never."

We know what heat is and we know what cold is. He said that while the earth remains there will always be a seedtime and a harvest time, there will be cold, and there will be heat. There will be summer, there will be winter, there will be day and there will be night. If we still have day and night then we still have seedtime and harvest time.

Now the nature of seedtime and harvest time is very simple. There's a time to plant seed and there's a time to reap your harvest. We understand from a natural perspective that if you plant your seed on Tuesday, you don't expect to reap your harvest on Wednesday. We know there's a period of time that you would go through— or an "expectancy period" where your harvest would come. During that time you would water your crops, tend to them, and pull out any weeds. You'll make sure that the environment (the condition in which the seed is planted) is right so it has the ability to continue to be fertilized to bring it into its fullest capacity.

So if seedtime and harvest still remain today and if we are to understand prosperity then you have to know the difference between a seed and its harvest. The reality is this; you are living in your harvest. "Well I don't see the fruit of this harvest." That's the harvest you're living in, the harvest of no fruit because you will produce whatever it is you have sown. So if you're saying, "Well I don't seem to have enough." then you don't plant enough. It's very simple.

I think we, as Christians, make it not only complicated, but unnecessarily complicated. If I'm a farmer and I look at my cornfields and say, "This is just not enough corn," your natural answer to me would be, "Plant more and you will get more. That which you did plant, you'd better be watering it and pulling out all the weeds. Take care of what you've planted so that when it produces you will get the maximum yield from it."

My grandfather lived in a part of Philadelphia where there had been multiple houses that were torn down. His house still remained so he had a lot of vacant land around him. It did not necessarily belong to him, but he took care of it because the city would not. So he used to plant and put gardens in various spots in that open land. There was a cherry tree, a blackberry bush, a grapevine— all kinds of vegetation (even though we were in the city).

When I stayed at my grandparents' house, I had the opportunity to plant a garden with him. Now the interesting thing is this; to the natural eye as a young kid, the ground looked exactly the rake to turn up the ground and create rows. Then, we'd plant the seed, push the dirt back into the ground, and next thing you know the ground would look exactly the same as it did before we started.

I mentioned that memory because I want you to understand that often times when you plant seeds, your circumstances will look exactly the same as they did prior to you planting the seed. If you are impatient then you will observe the ground and think, "Well maybe this does not work." This is what Christians often do concerning their seed.

In a natural agrarian system you have to be careful, especially of pests. When we planted strawberries, we would put a little chicken wire cage underneath and all the way around the strawberry plants because there were gophers and moles, which — if you didn't know — gophers and moles love strawberries. The chicken wire was there to inhibit their ability to burrow under or climb up to reach the strawberries from the top. See, pests will destroy your harvest. So you, as a wise farmer who understands seedtime and harvest, would have to apply the same understanding of what we know naturally to the same thing spiritually.

In other words, there's a pest who's always after your fruit and if you don't have the ability to place armor around your seed then he will take it at any turn of events because he comes to steal, to kill and to destroy. The Bible tells us to put on the whole armor of God because if you don't have any armor then the devil walks in whenever he wants to and begins to devour your harvest.

Water is required to produce a harvest. We understand the water to be the Word. So if you sow a seed of destruction amongst your seeds of prosperity by allowing your mouth to say things like, "Well I guess this didn't work," you've just sown a seed, but that seed will grow up as a weed and choke out the seed of prosperity that you've planted. What does a farmer do with a weed? He pulls it out because the weed grows faster than the plant does. Anything that grows faster than your plant will require more energy than your plant will absorb. That's why weeds have to go.

When you plant seeds of doubt, unbelief and fear, these types of seeds grow faster than others because they line up with your feelings. As you give heed to it and faith to it, it grows faster than your plant and if you don't uproot it, it will choke out the seed that you've sown. You have to pull every weed, then you have to water your seed with the Word by speaking the Word over it.

I want you to understand that every time you plant a seed you have to pull every weed. You have to protect and water it with the Word or else it will not grow. Every single time someone says to me, *"Pastor I've been giving but I'm not prospering,"* I can tell you it's one of three things. They have spoiled their seed by speaking negativity over it, they forgot their seed was in the ground so they stopped speaking the Word over it and watering it, or they forgot to protect it and Satan stole it.

I can assure you of one thing— every seed shall produce something. The question is not whether your seed *will* produce, the question is will your seed produce for *you?* There are people that ask things like, "Should we expect a harvest from our seed?" If I was a farmer and I planted a multitude of seed but I looked at you and said, "I don't expect any of that to grow but I bought all of it. I spent days and days planting it but I don't expect it to grow." It does not even sound right.

Now, you do not give to receive, but you must understand that when you give, receiving comes with it. People struggle financially because they are reaping what they have sown. If sown little, they reap little. Everything that you reap is the byproduct of what you have sown. How have you sown your seed? Years ago when you were in Macy's and were offered that "free" credit card (or what you thought was a free credit card that you're still paying off to this day) and you decided to buy more instead of save, you have sown something. The realities are that until we take responsibility for what we have sown, *we will never reap.*

People amaze me at how they struggle with different things yet never recognize their fault in it. How do we change, how do we grow, how do we prosper if we are unwilling and unable to say we did this and this is the fruit (or the harvest) off of something we planted? Now the beautiful part is that God is a forgiving God. You can come to Him and He will turn it all around, but what happens to the Entitlement Generation is that they think if it takes too long then it's not worth it so it never gets turned around. You then have people who mismanage their money at 16, they mismanage their money at 26, then they mismanage their money at 46 and 66, and so on. All because nothing has ever changed in their understanding of this simple concept: you will reap exactly what it is that you've sown.

Genesis 1:11
"And God said, Let the earth bring forth grass, the herb yielding seed, and the fruit tree yielding fruit after his kind, whose seed is in itself, upon the earth: and it was so. And the earth brought forth grass, and herb yielding seed after his kind, and the tree yielding fruit, whose seed was in itself, after his kind: and God saw that it was good."

What type of seed is produced from a tree? Whatever kind of tree it is! God says the ability to reproduce is in the seed. Any idiot can tell me how many seeds are in an apple but only God can tell you how many apples are in one seed. Inside of the seed is the ability for the seed to reproduce itself.

Let's say I gave someone an apple to hold. As long as he holds onto the apple and does not put it in the ground, it is his and it's just increase. However, the moment he takes the increase (the apple) and plants it, it now becomes seed. In this seed is the ability for it to reproduce itself. I'm not even talking about anything supernatural right now, I'm just talking about a natural understanding that a seed has to fall to the ground and die in order for whatever's in it to produce. In it has its very nature of reproduction.

If you are the smartest person in the world or dumber than a box of rocks, as long as you take this and plant it, it will produce. The seed does not have the ability to be selective based on race, gender, or ethnicity. It does not have the ability to select who it produces for, it just produces. And it produces after its own kind. The Bible tells us that every tree produces after its own kind. If I plant an apple tree or apple seeds, I will grow an apple tree. If I plant orange seeds, I will grow an orange tree, so it will produce after its own kind.

So if my seed is a dollar then I will reap the potential in this dollar as seed. If my seed is a million dollars, I will reap the potential of a million dollars because in the very seed is the nature for it to reproduce. All I have to do is plant it.

I have a friend (she's an Assistant Pastor) who was in Africa one time and she saw a bag of seeds sitting on a table. She approached a man about this bag and said, "Could I have some of these?" The guy was perplexed so he asked, "What do you want them for?" She said, "Oh they looked like seeds I wanted to taste them." He responded by saying, "No, around here we don't eat our

When you take your seed to Starbucks, you just ate it. When you take your seed and refuse to tithe, you just ate it. You did not plant it, you ate it. The man told her they don't eat their seed because they were in severe famine, and they understand that every single seed may be good for nourishment. If I plant the seed it has the potential to feed more than just me. It works the same way spiritually; when you eat your seed it has the potential to nourish you but everything God does is not just to bless you— that's why he said you're blessed to be a *blessing* (Genesis 12:2).

I do not know why I have such a hard time getting that one point across— that you're blessed to be a blessing. You are not blessed to warm the chair at church and think that everyone else is supposed to be excited just because you showed up. You are not blessed with financial wealth so that you can have such a great home and vehicles and boats and enjoy them on Sunday instead of going to church. You are blessed, empowered to prosper, to be a blessing and empower others to prosper. The challenge is that when you talk about seedtime and harvest, what I think we don't realize is that as long as this dollar circulates in the secular world, it will never produce a harvest for God. Satan's plan is to keep you circulating seed into the hands of APS, into your mortgage holder's hands, into Starbucks' hands. Go down to Wally World and put it in their hands. Go down to the more expensive Wally World (which is Target) and put it in their hands. Yet and still the ability for this seed to produce is still in itself. I need you to know that because it helps you recognize where you put your money.

My money does not go everywhere because I understand seedtime and harvest. I understand that every dollar, every nickel, everything that I turn over, whatever I put it in, it in itself has the ability to produce. Now the question is who is it going to produce for? Is it going to produce for Satan, or is it going to produce for

7

God? This is a very serious discussion to have with yourself to say, "As soon as the seed leaves my hands, it's going to be planted somewhere. Where am I putting all of my money?" Paul said, "I pray that your treasure would abound in Heaven."

Whatever you do here translates to your Heavenly account. Where do you put the majority of your finances? How do you spend the majority of your seed? How much of your seed are you actually eating? If seedtime and harvest time still remains and what I'm telling you is biblical, then if you're not walking in the harvest that you were expecting, you have to inspect what you planted; that's if you've planted at all! Then you are going through famine and wondering, "How did I get here?"

See, your job is not your source. Your job is to provide you with seed. God is your source, He expects to be your provider, He expects to be your deliverer, your rock, the source of your prosperity. So why do you have a job? You have one to receive seed so that when you plant, God giveth increase and you prosper. Do you know how many people have that mixed up? They think the job is their supply. It's not, and this is why people will submit themselves to unreasonable men. An unreasonable man will say, "I know I told you that you can have Sundays off, but things have changed." My response would be, "If things have changed, see you later. My God never changes and this is not my supply. God is my supply. If this has to change then I have to change."

It seems we don't want to set bars anymore because the reality is we're afraid God won't answer. We play that, what I call "Safe Christianity" that says we'll be Christian enough that in the event a trumpet blows and He comes in the clouds all of a sudden, we can get right." If you are truly at a place where you trust God then you will stand in the face of any situation and say, "I will not do that. I will not lie, cheat, steal or deal with unreasonable men because my God is really my supply. You, job, happen to be God's conduit."

Now, adversely there are people who think they're entitled to everything. They go to work thinking, "I showed up so I should get paid." *You're blessed to be a blessing.* You're blessed to bring a supply, so what you're supposed to do is bring a supply. Here's something I've learned— I'm telling you this is a fact; when you are needed in an organization, they will do whatever it takes to keep you. If you are obsolete (meaning: you love texting on the phone when you should be working. You love calling your friends instead of working) do not expect to stick around. You are there to work — to be a blessing, as you're getting blessed.

God said that "the blessing of the Lord is what maketh rich and adds no sorrow to it" (Proverbs 10:22). So my responsibility is to show up and bring my supply in everything that I do, then money cometh because I'm planting seed.

I don't worry about what people are going to give me. I concern myself with what I can give to them because I'm absolutely certain that the harvest I'm walking in today was because of seeds that I've sown years ago: seeds of faithfulness, seeds of commitment, seeds of keeping my mouth shut, seeds of serving wherever I needed to serve, and understanding how to bring my supply without complaining about everything because it did not fit my needs.

See I understood that, and that's why I planted those seeds. I planted seeds financially by giving and tithing— and I didn't just tithe but I gave offering. I understood (not back then, but now) that those seeds are what took this ministry and established it when I had nothing. Those seeds are what caused a pastor in Mesa to call me and say, "Hey I need you to come look at some stuff," then that man to call me and say, "Hey I've got 200 chairs, you want them? We just bought them but we don't need them anymore." Seedtime and harvest time, and the spirit of stinginess will always keep you from planting seed because you will calculate the situation.

Ecclesiastes 11:5
"As thou knowest not what is the way of the spirit, nor how the bones do grow in the womb of her that is with child: even so thou knowest not the works of God who maketh all."

We have to understand how spiritual things work. Really, you probably don't understand how a child grows in the womb, so because you don't understand that, he likens that to how the spirit functions and operates. You may not yet know that the child is growing in the womb but it does. Do you know exactly how a child is conceived and the exact process by which that grows? No, but you know what happens or else you wouldn't be here. That's the essence of faith is to know that something happens that may not be to your understanding, it may not be within your realm of comprehension but you know that it still happens anyway.

If you want it to happen, do not want it to happen, do not like that it happened, do not care that it happens, or you really wish that it did not happen, it still happened. That's what he said, that's the way of the Spirit. You don't know exactly how it happens, but God does. He said it happens anyway. This is why people can lose their seed because they think if they do not see it, if they've not the ability to climb up in the womb and start growing the baby themselves, then it's not going to happen.

I'm not talking about natural things, but spiritual things. Do you want to know 10 ways to naturally become a millionaire? Go buy one of the multitude of books that everybody has written on how to become a millionaire (who were not millionaires when they wrote the book but are now by duping you into buying the book). If you want that, I cannot do anything for you, but if you want to understand how God can prosper you, then there's only one way that it works and it's by faith.

You have to walk by faith, breathe by faith, talk by faith, act by faith, move by faith, and become a person of faith. Faith does not know how it gets done, but it knows it will be done.

So when he says you don't even know how it grows in the womb, I don't need to know how. Here's what I know; if I want a harvest, I have to sow a seed. Not only do I require seed, but I have to put that seed in the ground because if I put it in Starbucks, my harvest is that cup of coffee. In natural transactional relationships, I give you one thing in exchange for another. I have received my harvest.

Starbucks will not call you two months from now to say, "You remember that five dollars you paid for that caramel maccchiato mocha latte skim with the whip cream, milk and caramel topping with the extra pump of who knows what? Well, it produced another one so tomorrow would you come pickup the second one?" However, with God every seed you plant, as long as you're willing to continue to water it with the Word, remove any weeds of doubt, and stay at a place where you are expecting production, it will continue to produce over and over again. Your bank account might pay you a percent but God is into multiplication and you have to learn that the seed itself has the ability to produce. Wherever you put it is where it will produce.

Think about the very nature of a business. You know what the whole premise of a business is? To hire you for less than what you produce so they become profitable. Let's say on a yearly basis you bring in $100,000 to the company. If I'm the business, my goal is to pay you $50,000 so now I make $50,000 off of you. You are paid less than what you produce because that margin is the profit for the organization. That's why in the olden days you used to find people that were butchers, bakers and candlestick makers. They all had trades, they made all of their money. Somewhere in the last couple hundred years we've been convinced to go with what's safe. We make less, but at least we know we have a job to go to every single day. We become cogs in the wheel of commerce not realizing that we really are being pimped.

The goal is to pay you as little as possible while getting as much out of you as possible. If you are being paid what you produce, you will be fired pretty soon. If you are producing less than what you are paid, you probably have already been fired. It's business, it's spreadsheet management. You look at a spreadsheet and see what each person produces, asking the key questions: What's the cost of it? How much do we pay them? What is it really worth? Does this line up?

If we're paying them less than what they're really worth, we keep them. If they're not doing the job, if they show up for eight hours and we only have one hour of work out of them, hit the road Jack. That's how it works. This is the sad part but some people spend 25-30 years and they received pay raises that have placed them at a point where the business could hire two young people to replace them and could pay them less... and then we wonder why so many people are laid off.

It's the same principle with your money and I want you to recognize that when you work 9-5, when you are paid $20 an hour you are tit-for-tat. 1 hour of work equates to $20. There's no multiplication in that, it's transactional. I'm not telling you to quit your job, but if you want to prosper beyond tit-for-tat, you'd better how to acquire some supernatural assistance because otherwise you will never be paid what you are worth. Yes, you can chase after the world's system all you want to, but the world's system is designed to never let you move ahead because you don't understand money. Wealthy people understand money, that's why they put their money in investments.

So, what's the difference between spending versus making an investment? Spending is 1:1. If I give you $500 you give me an iPad; it's transactional. I send you $100, you send me this product. Investments go beyond the initial transaction because you've planted a seed naturally into a stock, a bond, a mutual fund, real estate, or whatever it may be. How much more would you gain if you were to understand that God's account is your investment account?

I don't know of anybody that's knocked over the First Bank of God. I have not heard that He went bankrupt or that there's some CEO in Heaven stealing the money, but how come we don't think like that? Why don't we recognize that we could take the time to make investments into what God is doing? We treat it in our heads like we lost or spent money. If seed really has the ability to produce in and of itself, then if I plant it or invest it, it will bring a greater degree of return than if I transactionally spent it.

I recognize that I could either spend it or I can invest it. If I invest it, I'm sowing it and as long as the Earth remains there shall be seedtime and harvest time. I may not be able to look at it and see how it grows or how it happens. I cannot tell you, but here's what I can tell you; I was once blind, now I can see. How I got from here to there, couldn't tell you. I probably make in a year what I used to make in a month and now I have no debt. I don't have the stress levels I used to have. I have a better wardrobe, a nicer house. How does that happen? I cannot tell you.

If you wanted me to tell you specifically how that all transpired, how I have more peace than I did then, how things are always supplied, how I lack for nothing, everything I need is fully supplied, fully funded. I couldn't tell you how that happens logistically. All I can tell you is that every chance I have I'm putting seed in the ground. I'm planting into the ministry, into people's lives and I'm sowing whatever I can. I call it bringing my supply.

If the Bible says I'm supplied by the supply I bring in Ephesians, that means that if I bring everything that I have as a supply then that means I receive. This is why people struggle. They don't bring their supply. They talk about their supply, they're quick to tell you, "Oh I'm a prophet. I'm an Apostle to the nations." How many churches have you started? "Well, none." You're an Apostle to who and to what? "Well I'm called to be this." Where's your fruit? If you are called to do something then you should be producing fruit and that's how you bring your supply. Not to the world; because the world is transactional.

Some of you are very good at bringing your supply to the job. You are the best at what you do in that job, but you go into the church and do absolutely nothing, never stopping to think to yourself, "Is God really pleased with that?" Did He set you up with all your skills, abilities, talents, giftings and treasures for you to just keep that chair warm? Seedtime and harvest; you reap what you sow. The Bible tells us be not deceived (Galatians 6:7). In other words, don't lie to yourself. All deception begins because the person who is spreading deception has been deceived. He's saying don't you lie to yourself, "God will not be mocked. That which you sow," the Amplified says, "And that only shall you reap." If seedtime and harvest always remain then do we ever come to the understanding that the very thing you are harvesting now, you've

People complain sometimes that their children are bad. Do you ever stop to think that child is a reflection of you? You may say, "Well that child is bad." but did you ever stop and think that the child looks like you? Be not deceived, God will not be mocked. That which you sow you shall also reap.

One day, I was on Facebook, and last minute a radio station called KXEG called to ask if we would speak on their station. We were talking about the ministry and different things. In between taping, she was talking about churches that have a problem with the Sinner's Prayer and how they don't like it. They feel it's unscriptural because you don't have to confess your sins. Hebrews 4 lays out some of the doctrines of Christ; one of the doctrines of Christ is repentance. This hyper-grace message has gone against the idea of repentance, creating a mindset that everything works like a "get out of jail free" card from the game Monopoly. Don't get me wrong, the grace of God is present and the grace of God will do things for you that you obviously just don't deserve, but if you deceive yourself into believing you can violate spiritual laws without facing the consequences of it, you have lied to yourself.

I don't care how much hyper-grace you preach, I don't care how much you want to think we're all multi-billionaires, or you believe that nonsense on TV; if you think that you will not have to be responsible for this life, I don't know that gospel. I don't know that I've ever even heard that gospel in its entirety. What I know is "be not deceived," which means you might be deceived by something but God will not be mocked. I also know that you have to be willing to take inventory. You have to look at what do you do with your seed and be honest.

If you eat it that's where your seed's going. If you're bringing your supply, you're planting seed. You will be supplied by the supply that you bring. You will find that any relationship that does have equity or reciprocity will be destroyed. If you are in a relationship, husband and wife, and the wife does not bring anything to the husband (or vice versa, if the husband won't bring anything to the wife) that relationship will not last.

In the same way, I wonder how we began to think that God's relationship with us is only one way. Every relationship that does not have a level of reciprocity dies. You want to prosper? Put God first. I say this with absolute conviction and I am assured to tell you, you want to learn how to prosper? Put God first. What happened to the people who understood we have to put God first? I don't have any other choice. I'm in too deep. That's what keeps me afloat, that's what keeps me living and breathing, that's what keeps everything going for me.

I don't know how to do it anymore. How about you? Or are you still at that place of the lie that says if I had it I'd do it? You do not have it because you refuse to do it and that's why. You have to learn the concept of seedtime and harvest! You have to look at everything that comes through your hands because it has the ability to reproduce itself. If it's in your hands, you now have a choice. Do you spend it, or do you invest it? Do you eat it, or do you plant it? The Bible tells us that he who observes the wind will not plant. He who observes the circumstances, the situations; you walk out of your house, "Oh it's going to thunderstorm today, I won't plant today." Satan will always use circumstances to prevent you from planting if that's who you are. That's why something pops up; to keep you from sowing.

You have to know that the choice is always yours. I want you to honestly think about this; every time seed is in your hands, I want you to think, "Am I going to spend it or am I going to invest it? Am I going to sow?" I'm not condoning you to invest all of your money and have nothing by which to live. Do I believe if you did that, God would take care of you? Of course I do, but I don't believe everyone has faith for that. What'll happen is when you fall you'll blame God or you'll blame me! I'm used to being blamed so I couldn't care less, but I don't want you to blame God because the only answer you'll ever have is God.

However, I want you to think about what you have and what you are doing with it. Are you sowing it, or are you eating it? Are you planting it? Are you investing it? What are you doing? In the very nature of what you have, it has the ability to produce in and of itself and spiritually, every seed will produce.

Do you want to have good friendships? Be a good friend. The reason why you have bad friends is because birds of a feather flock together. You complain, "I hate my friends, they're the worst." Well somewhere along the line that mirror has to swing back around because if those are the people that are attracted to you, you have to ask yourself what vibe are you putting off?

"Oh I always get the worst guys, I just choose the worst people." What is it about you that they like? Do you live above your means? Are you one of those people that has to have what the Jones' have? Let me tell you, it's expensive keeping up with the Jones'. The difference between you and the Jones' is they don't have spiritual resistance because they're not doing anything for God. That's why the Jones' make it look so good. However, I guarantee you when you reach Heaven you might be wondering, "Hey, where are the Jones' at?" At that moment you will come to the shocking realization that all the things the Jones' thought was important, were not.

Make wise decisions, make wise choices. I promise you, if you apply half of what I'm telling you, you will see the increase that God will bring into your life and people will even become jealous of it. People will become envious, even your self-professed Christian brothers and sisters. Unmistakably and undeniably, haters are always the mark of success and if everybody likes you, you're not doing much. You'll know that you're doing things for God when people start to turn on you. That's when you'll know you're doing something because you are rubbing people the wrong way.

I don't mean that in a bad way, I mean that in a good way. I want— my heart, my honest to goodness heart— is for you to prosper. I want you blessed going in and blessed going out. Why? The fruit in you reflects what I've given and fed to you. For you to do business with it is a jewel in my crown. For you to be successful is a mark in my win category. I don't want for you to struggle. I cannot tell you or anyone that all you do is wait upon the Lord and they who wait will mount up with wings.

I could do that, but the reality is I honestly want for you to gain an understanding because when you understand it, you can apply it for yourself, then turn around and help others. I'm working off the fruit concept. I couldn't care less whether you like me, think I'm handsome, or whatever is your opinion of me. What I want you to do is grow, be stretched, learn the ways of God, and not just the acts of God. When you learn God's ways, people will look at you and ask, "How is it that you do less and have more?"

Your ability to do less and have more is a sign of the anointing; that's what the anointing is for.

GROWING
Guarding Your Seed

Mark 4:26-32

"And he said, So is the kingdom of God, as if a man should cast seed into the ground; And should sleep, and rise night and day, and the seed should spring and grow up, he knoweth not how. For the earth bringeth forth fruit of herself; first the blade, then the ear, after that the full corn in the ear. But when the fruit is brought forth, immediately he putteth in the sickle, because the harvest is come. And he said, Whereunto shall we liken the kingdom of God? or with what comparison shall we compare it? It is like a grain of mustard seed, which, when it is sown in the earth, is less than all the seeds that be in the earth: But when it is sown, it groweth up, and becometh greater than all herbs, and shooteth out great branches; so that the fowls of the air may lodge under the shadow of it."

We don't know every detail of how things grow in the ground, we don't know every detail of how a baby grows in the womb, but we know that it happens. Although we are not intimately involved in the process of that child developing (it's not in our hands that it happens) we just know that it happens and we trust that it happens. We have faith that it happens. There's a point after gestation and a period of growth that the child is born. Of course we celebrate that, and we're excited about that because if we could parallel that into agricultural terms we would say that the harvest has now come.

Afterall, the time between planting and reaping is a process of gestation, or a time of growth. You don't necessarily know how it happens but that it is happening. What he's saying in this verse is that when you have planted a seed, it's like a mustard seed. A mustard seed is a very small seed, but when it's planted in good soil it will produce branches and leaves that will provide birds with a cover they'll be able to hide underneath.

He also says that there's a process where first you have the blade, then you have the ear, then after you have the full corn in the ear. This passage of scripture speaks to progression, growth and development.

It is amazing to me how people want to prosper. They're enamored with the idea that they want to prosper; they want to drive nice cars, they want to have nice things, and they want to live in a nice house. Of course, I'm not saying that these things shouldn't be a desire for you, but if you don't understand the concepts of planting you will never walk in the fullness of what God has for you. You'll be able to receive what you can produce out of your own hands but if you want more than what you're able to do, you have to subscribe to some biblical principles. It's amazing to me that the same people I see who are the cheapest are often the ones who struggle the most. The world of the stingy gets smaller and smaller, but the world of the generous gets bigger (Proverbs 11:24).

How is that possible? It's because there's a biblical principle that comes with seedtime and harvest time! It seems that when most people are planting seed, they do not realize that it is a timely process. If you are expecting a very small harvest, you will reap it very quickly. There are some people who do things and want everybody to see it. They plant a seed and try to make sure everybody can see it. This way they're receiving glory others are enamored by the idea of such a large seed being planted. When you do this, you receive your reward very quickly.

When you are truly planting seed, first of all nobody needs to know what you've done. Secondly, if you're holding fast to your profession then when you eventually see the first blade come up, you'll see the ear come up next, and then you'll see the full corn in the ear. You'll see a full process of growth and development that will bring you to a place that you're actually ready to put forth into a sickle.

Some people, because they don't have patience, will come and try to take the harvest before there's any corn in the ear. Some will eat the blade of grass because of their impatience instead of waiting for the full corn. I don't know if you've ever tasted grass but grass is nasty; I'd rather have the corn! However, the corn takes patience and faith. He likened it to the Kingdom of God. He said whatever is planted that is Kingdom-purposed will produce a harvest in your life, but you have to be patient.

You have to allow it to go through its full process of development. If you're expecting an oak tree and you planted an acorn, you cannot wake up tomorrow and say, "Where's my oak tree?" What Satan will use as the biggest dream-killer and vision thief, is your time. Uniquely time is your largest ally and asset. The biggest trick Satan has you to believe is that you don't have it, when the reality is that you have all the time God needs you to have.

When you become impatient you want everything and you want it right now. Faith is holding fast to a profession. Faith is not something that is in you one day and gone the next. Faith is something that you absolutely have to maintain on a daily basis. You have to make sure to continue to speak faith over whatever met. I know that I've planted this seed and some will reap 30, some 60 and some 100 fold but I'm going to reap 100 fold. I'm going to be patient enough to wait and to know that God has got me. In any situation, I am ready to stand boldly and declare that I know my God is well able no matter what the circumstances look like and the situation looks like..." Sadly, this is where people struggle.

The Bible tells us that a man that can control their mouth can control every other part of their body. The first thing people say is, "Well you know I don't have enough to tithe and if I did I would." That's why you don't. 10% is a quantitive number. It's a specific number based on what you have, so if you have $5, ten percent is still ten percent. If you have a million dollars, ten percent is still ten percent. God is not interested in the dollar amount, He's interested in the ten percent because it's the tithe, it's holy unto God. It is not for you to eat, it is not for you to withhold. It is not for you to think, "One day I'll be able to do this."

Once we accept tithing, let's talk about offering. There are a lot of people that give exactly what their tithe is. I've watched too many people lose their job and then come to me wondering why they lost it. The answer is simple, it became an idol. The job became more important than God. The job became more interesting to them than the things of God and it became an idol. Once it becomes an idol, once it stops you from doing the things that you would normally do in the service of your God, it's an idol for you.

We run through our lives looking at the job and material possessions as our source and we forget that God is the source! So if you want more than what you're already getting, you have to do something different than what you've already done. I know some of you reading this are wondering "Well Pastor, do you just want our money?" No, I couldn't care less. You are not my source. God's

He prospers me and even if I were in a tin can hiding in a rooftop somewhere, He'd still prosper me because that's my relationship with Him. I give, I sow. When I see opportunities, I take them but it's not about a ten percent tithe only, it's about recognizing that if you are generous, if that's your personality, then you're going to be generous. You're not going to be counting money all of the time. Everything's not about how you can turn a profit out of the situation.

I'm talking about some real important things because that which you sow, you will reap. The areas in which you don't sow, you will reap nothing. If you sow nothing, you reap nothing; and that's the sad part about sowing and reaping. You really will get what you give and if you give little, you get little. It's really that simple and when people struggle with their finances the first thing I want to know is are you a giver?

I'm pretty far removed now from the process of knowing who gives what, who tithes and who does not tithe. I like that. I don't ever want you to think I'm speaking directly to you. I don't know which person in the congregation tithes and which person does not tithe anymore. I don't even know that I really care. Here's what I do know: I can usually come up with 100% accuracy as to why the ones who are struggling are not walking in the prosperity that God wants for them. You want to know what it is? They don't have enough seed in the ground.

Naturally, if we were talking to a farmer and the farmer said, "I'm really tired, my harvest is just too small." I think you would naturally ask him, "How much seed did you plant?" If he said, "Well I only planted a little bit." Would you then be upset, go into the field and pray to God and tell Him, "God I pray the harvest comes…" Why would you do that? You already know the problem is in the natural. He's not planted enough seed. If he did not plant the proper amount of seed then his faith level is pretty low, which means he wasn't expecting much and that's why he planted little.

When we look at our finances and the things we do financially, if you're expecting something big from God, then you'd better be sowing something big. It's not that God's punishing you, it's an exercise of your faith. When you are at a place where you're able to sow generously into the kingdom you will see what I'm talking about I guarantee it. This is not something that I've made up, this is something I've lived. It's not just about money, it's about how you treat the things of God. You're asked to do something, you're involved in a ministry but you cannot show up, help out, bring your supply; you're always causing problems and troubles, and people have to chase you down.

You're not really doing what you've been asked to do, you're causing harm to the body. That which you sow you shall reap. If you're not handling things well, if you're not being skillful you will reap it. People want the prosperity of God, they want the blessings of God, but none of the responsibilities. To be honest with you it's childish because I'm not going to sit here and tell you that if you just pray God's going to bless you will a million dollars. That is not the prosperity message I know.

I'm not going to tell you if you give according to Psalms 66, if you give me $66 God will bless you with a million. You will not hear that from me. What I'm going to tell you is this; If you continue to sow seed by faith you will reap a harvest. If you are skillful with the things of God, you respect the house of God, you respect the things you've been asked to do no matter how great or small, you will be successful. If you don't do those things, you will not be successful and great will be the fall of it. Just a matter of time.

My goal is to offend your mind to reveal your heart. Everything in your life reflects seedtime and harvest. Your children reflect seedtime and harvest. You might be wondering, "How can my child be so disrespectful to me?" Seedtime and harvest. "How can this happen this way?" Seedtime and harvest. "How is it that I'm not being promoted on my job?" Seedtime and harvest. "How come I'm not being promoted at church?" Seedtime and harvest. The Bible says, "Be not deceived." In other words, don't lie to yourself.

Deception always begins with the person speaking deception being deceived. A lot of people will lie to themselves. How do we ever experience real prosperity? I don't mean a financial number. When I say to you I'm prosperous, what I'm telling you is that my body is healed and whole, my presses burst out with new wine, every enterprise that I put my hands to will prosper and it does not have a choice. What I'm telling you is that everything that I need shall be supplied.

Now whatever quantitive number that becomes, whether it's a million or a hundred dollars is not my concern nor is it my issue. How do you gain that level of confidence? You need to have some seed in the ground. I'm constantly seeking opportunities to put seed in the ground whether or not it's money. It might be I know someone has a personal goal and I'm going to make it my mission to help them accomplish it. People don't recognize that the way they handle things determines the seedtime and a harvest time.

You will reap what you've sown. If you have sown well and then you belabor the weeds into what you've done, the weeds will choke out your seed and you'll lose it. You don't have the luxury of sitting around complaining about your financial situation. "Well I planted seed, I sowed, I gave and nothing happened." The moment you open your mouth like that you set your field on fire. All that questioning is setting your field on fire because you have not learned how to curb your mouth. That's why the Bible says, "How great a fire such a little member can kindle." Meanwhile, as your field burns you're wondering, "What happened?" Then you blame God. Christians particularly, one of the things that I think we have lost is our sensibility. We want to keep up with the Jones'. If the Jones' have a brand new this, we need a brand new that. If they have a bigger house, we need a better car. Never mind that our finances have not caught up with us. When you're stretched in your faith, you need enough faith to get there. What people will do is they will desire things of their heart that God was willing to bless them with but they are out beyond their soul.

They are beyond their ability to believe God for it. If you are living in a house and it costs you $1,000 a month it might not be a good idea for you to acquire another $3,000-$4,000 payment. You're a fool if you say, "Well I've got faith, I'm believing God!" I've been there. The thing about it is they don't care, they want it every single month. The payment comes around with amazing regularity. If your faith is not at that place, this is what you may have done. You have asked, "Why am I struggling?" It's because you have pushed beyond what you can believe God for. Now you're out there by yourself.

Can God do it? Of course He can, but He works with you according to the power that works within you. If you can't believe God for it then you're out in a place where you should not be. I'm not trying to tell you that everybody's going to be a millionaire. What I'm trying to do is give you sound, doctrinal principles that will help you. When Paul said, "I was pressed beyond my measure insomuch that we wanted to die" (2 Corinthians 1:8) he was saying he moved out beyond the measure God gave him. It wasn't that God couldn't save him or deliver him, it was the fact that he was beyond his measure. As he moved beyond his measure, things became worse and worse. God did not change, God did not weaken or lose His power; he was beyond the measure that God had given him that he was able to believe for.

We also know that he penned the words that said, "This is but a light affliction" (2 Corinthians 4:17). How was he able to say it was a light affliction? It was within his measure. We've gotten to a place where we're trying to keep up with the Jones'. If they have a new iPad 6 then we need one also. Never mind the fact that the one you already have works just as well. Now you're out there getting yourself in debt to have the latest iPhone 63 because everybody else has one. It's a lack of wisdom and it's ridiculous. It seems we act like the world and wonder why we achieve worldly results.

The Bible tells us that which we sow we shall reap, so if we sow stupidity we will reap stupidity. I want you to be successful, to be people that can walk in the prosperity of God. I want you to understand that it is not on God's end that you are not prospering. He's already done all He had to do. If you are not walking in what God has for you, it's on your end. Maybe your faith level isn't high enough and that's fine, so back down a little bit. Come down to a place where you can believe God for it and stay there for awhile. If you're believing God for a Bentley back down to a Hugo or something. Build your faith up for a Ford Focus and start there. Once you have the Ford Focus lets step up.

These are practical things because what people will do in their Christianity is make silly and poor decisions, but they'll call it faith. There's a book written by Fred Price that's called *Faith of Foolishness* and I'm telling you, we as the body have to learn how to really be in faith. How do you know when you're in faith? You're not complaining. If you are complaining about your situation or something you're going through, you are not in faith about it.

Here's the beautiful part, we have the Word of God that you can delve into until you are in faith. Then when you are in faith, you move out by faith. What most people will do is move out by desire and then wish to be saved by faith. Once you're already drowning, "Oh God, help me!" That which you sow you shall surely reap. The question becomes for you, how do you manage what you sow?

I have five bank accounts and I know what's in each of them because they belong to me. I watch them. How many accounts do you have where you've sown into your account, you're supposed to be getting interest on it, but you forgot all about it? You're not even paying attention to it anymore, you don't even know what's in that account, you don't even know what you've sown. Then you're wondering why your harvest is not coming. All the while Satan has kept ledgers of everything you've done and while you're not paying attention he's robbing coffers blind. Then you turn to God and say, "God bless me." God is looking at you saying, "Really? You planted, I gave increase, what happened?"

This is a whole different prosperity book, isn't it? It's not one of those, "Give $66 and you'll get $50 million." It is not on God's end that the body of Christ is walking below the revelation line. If you had a million dollars and I said, "Give me a million dollars or give me the life of your child," I hope you would give me the million dollars. (I was going to say that I think all of you would but I'm not going to say that. It's a different world we live in, but I hope all of you would!) How much more would your Father who withheld nothing from you, not even to the sparing of his own child, give to you? How much more does He desire to see you blessed, prospering, and walking in the fullness of what He has for you?

Some people have a call of God on their life, but are disrespectful towards it. That's one of the reasons why they're not ing in the prosperity they need to walk in. They want it but don't realize that God will never give it until it's committed to His kingdom. They don't understand that prosperity comes when they're able to be in tune and follow God's plan. When we're walking in the perfect will of God, that's where we'll will see provision and the great things we aspire to. This is when we look at somebody and say, "Oh my God they're good at something." They're good at it because they're in the perfect will of God.

The greatest level of the anointing ever seen is when you are in the perfect will of God. It looks easy when you're doing exactly what He told you to do and saying exactly what He's told you to say. In that moment you are so intertwined with the vision of God that there has to be provision because God foreordained it. That's why the Bible says, "Unless God builds the house they that build it labor in vain" (Psalm 127:1). If God built the house why would we have to labor?

Think about it for a minute. If God built the house, why would we labor to build it if He already built it? God constructs it in the realm of the spirit and needs you to follow, in the natural, what He has planned and constructed in the spirit. As you construct what is planned in the spirit, you fulfill God's blueprint.

In real estate when you build a new home, they have a system of draws. A draw is where you build a house and it has certain stages. When the ground is ready to be built upon and the foundation is laid, you hit that benchmark. After that, they give you another draw of money, let's say $50,000. Once the house is framed and the electricity is running, they come out to inspect it again and give you another $50,000. Based on benchmarks of construction, they supply what you need to continue on after you've reached a certain point. You don't get more until you have constructed in the natural realm what God has constructed in the natural realm what God has constructed in the realm of the spirit, and as you reach benchmarks your draws come.

For some people, their challenge is that they have no steps beyond the first stage because the job, family and/or school has tied them up, and they've completely disregarded the things of God. Now they're not progressing. They keep coming back to the bank looking for an advance and when their fruit is inspected, but they have not constructed in the natural that which God has built in the realm of the spirit. Then, because those two don't agree, Satan steals it.

Now every time they go to put their 2x4s up, Satan steals them, takes them to his house, and builds his little mansions because he's stealing from them all the time. This is why proficiency in the realm of the spirit is critical! This is why you have to know what you are doing. You can say and confess that you're a millionaire until your lips fall off, but I promise you if the work of God is not being manifested in your life, you will never make it by God's hands. You might make it but it will be by the empowerment of Satan and then he'll steal it from you.

We have to recognize that we must be skillful with the things of God. This is why people will say, "Oh that prosperity gospel is not true." What other good news could there possibly be if God does not want you to prosper emotionally, physically, health-wise and financially? What else could be good news? You're going to die? You're going to be sick the rest of your life? Is that good news?

So the Gospel is the good news. The good news is that your sins have been forgiven. Why do you need you sins forgiven? So you can prosper. Sin keeps you in the curse and that curse is what keeps you from prospering. So if I know that I've been delivered from that, then what does it mean? That which God has blessed can no longer be cursed. So if I understand seedtime and harvest then I realize that I would rather put my money into things that are God-ordained so that God will bring me a harvest that I will never obtain out of the stock market or that 0.02% from my savings account. Have you paid attention to the fact that your savings account usually charges you more in a monthly fee than what they put in it? It's a system and as Christians we're blithely unaware, running around saying, "Come Lord, come!" and not even realizing we're being robbed.

I remember, years ago, there was a very bad situation that happened in the church I was attending. One of the pastors really just went off the deep end. One of the things she had done was put some blank checks in front of the senior pastor for the rent. The checks had the right amount, but there was no name written on them. He wasn't really paying attention and he signed the checks. This went on for about six months at $2,500 a month. After six months, the property management company contacted the pastor and said, "We're going to be padlocking the doors in a week because you're six months behind on your rent."

She was taking the checks, putting her name on them after he'd signed, and depositing them into her account. The church was $14,000-$15,000 short on their rent. The pastor called me and said, "Hey this is what happened. I need you to come to the bank with me. We've got to get to the bottom of this and I would like your insight into what's going on." So we went to the bank and they opened an investigation.

Sadly, because he signed the checks there was nothing they could do about it. If she had replaced his name with hers, that would have been forgery, but because he signed a blank check there was nothing that could be done. So here was this church, in a week it was going to be shut down, and I proceeded to write him a check for $15,000 to help the church come out of that situation.

Here's my point, I made a decision that I was going to personally see to it that the church would always have what it needed. That was my goal, and I knew what God wanted me to do it. I knew He prospered me in a business to do it, so I did it. I wasn't talking about it, I didn't say, "Oh Pastor I'm with you, I'm behind you!" then never did anything. When you understand that you have a supply, you are not concerned about those things. Was $15,000 a lot of money? I don't know, you tell me. You think after I wrote it that I didn't think about it and panic? Do you not think it strange that 10 years later my God has met every single need that I've ever had? Do you think I am unaware that seedtime and harvest is real?

I didn't ask for it from the pastor and I don't need it from him. I didn't do it for him, I did it for God. He just happened to be the ground in which I planted. God is the one who brings the increase and I know that because I understood seedtime and harvest. I understood how to take responsibility for the work in which God planted me. It's funny how there are people that will send more money to other ministries than they will to the one they're planted. God planted you there, yet you don't feel the need to support it.

These people turn into what we call "spiritual vampires." They suck the blood out of the ministry then refuse to support it. See, I understood my supply and when I had the ability to do, I did. Every time, I was planting seeds for my future. It's not strange and it's no miracle to me that I walk in provision now because I've personally taken responsibility for what God has asked me to do. I know beyond a shadow of a doubt that I can stand before Him and say, "Everything you told me to give, I gave. Every situation or problem that I could effect I did."

I didn't look at my pastor and say, "Man, we just have to pray about it." That's the rhetoric of lying Christians. At what point do you reach in your pocket? James says what does it matter if you say you're going to pray for somebody but not give them clothes to keep them warm, or give them food to eat (James 2:15-17). However, you'll be pious enough to say, "I'll pray for you." All the while it is hurting your prosperity, not mine.

For some of you that are overseeing ministries, if you'd take some responsibility for it and say, "You know what? I'm going to do this as if I'm doing it unto God," you would see greater degrees of manifestations in your life because now you're handling things skillfully with God and He is well pleased. He takes pleasure in the prosperity of His servants, not His critics and coattail riders.

Do you know how difficult it is when you won't tithe and everybody else who does tithe has to pull that wagon with you in it? Do you know how difficult it becomes when you decide you can't do it because you're still in the wagon and everybody else who is tithing is pulling your weight? I know you may not like what I'm saying here— and there are about 50,000 other ministers that can pat you on the head and tell you what you are doing is okay— but I want to tell you the truth and I want to help you. The realities are that it is time to end the games people sometimes play where they are disrespectful towards the things of God but still expect to be blessed. You cannot spit in God's face and then expect Him to somehow smile and take it.

The Bible says that He went out like a lamb but He's coming back like a lion. You should be more mindful of how you handle your life and what God has asked you to do. You really need to think because that which you sow you shall reap. Of course, in the time of reaping the good things, everybody loves it. There's a huge celebration and people start declaring, "God's blessing me! I'm walking in it!" But the moment you reap what you don't want, there's wailing and complaining. I'm not sharing this to brag on what I did, but to let you know that when I had to figure out how to put food on my table and to build a church years ago, when I'm selling my possessions to keep the church going, there's a commitment that comes with the responsibility of understanding your supply. When you bring your supply, God takes care of you.

When you refuse to bring your supply, then you live based on what you have and that's why you have what you have. When was the last time you sacrificed something? When was the last time you did something that cost you? I'm not talking about giving away something that didn't mean much in the first place or doing something that is well within your ability to do. I'm talking about sowing a seed that cost you something.

It's easy to be comfortable. We can sit back and ride high on yesterday's blessing. However, what if the only thing(s) you had in your life today are the things you thanked God for yesterday? Some of you have not thanked God for anything and it's the reason you have nothing today. I want you to be successful and have the desires of your heart, but not at the expense of God. Your blessings are in the benefit for God because He has a kingdom to build and if you are a part of the kingdom building, you will find that you have more provision than you know what to do with.

Every time you invest, it'll keep coming back in because you're a part of the Kingdom, and you are doing Kingdom business. Some of you are doing your business and your secular worries, fears and concerns have nothing to do with God, but you still want to prosper. However, when you plant those seeds of apathy and discontent, why do you question your harvest when you reap nothing but apathy and discontent? So, I ask you again, when was the last time you sowed something that cost you? You've before that with no pain, there is no gain. So if there's been nothing ventured, how can you gain anything? At what point do we decide there has to be some truth to this?

For some people reading this, it's taken so long for you to understand it. For others, you may have businesses and are sowing, giving and doing everything you're supposed to do. For you, God's providing in an amazing way because of your obedience. However, for the ones that are not so obedient, you're finding this to be a constant struggle. It seems you always have to resort to something else. You continually decide that something else has to be your source. Whether it's drugs, alcohol, money, lust or desire; something else alway has to fill that void. That void is created when you're not walking in the perfect plan that God has for you.

It seems for some of you, there's always that empty space so you work harder to build something up, but I'm telling you that unless the Lord builds a house, he who builds it will labor in vain. Some of you are building a self-made tower, mansions and apartments unto yourself. However, if you will construct in the natural what God has already foreordained for your life in the realm of the spirit, you will see greater degrees of manifestation in your life. Everyone is building something, so the question has to be whether or not you're building according to the blueprint God has for you. If you are, you'll see greater help, greater healing, and provision in your life. It's not that hard and it's not a secret. God said if you lack wisdom, ask for it.

People often say, "I want to be in ministry," but it never fails; there are always some who claim to want this but can't seem to show up when it's time to work. It makes me wonder, "Where's the ministry at, in your house?" Some of us are living like this, yet we want to be prosperous. Why would God prosper you to be in your house and achieve nothing? Why would God prosper you to sit at home? He would need to equip you for something that He's asked you to do so that when you do it there's a supply present for you to accomplish it. Otherwise He would be a very mean God to ask you to do something that He wasn't going to pay or supply you with what's needed to do it. Don't you think so?

I don't think our God is unfair, unjust, unkind, or unloving. I think He knows exactly what He has need of.

How can Coca-Cola have the goal of being on every continent in the world and accomplish that in 25 years, yet we've been preaching the gospel for thousands of years and still can't seem to circle the globe? There are people who claim Christianity but deny its power. They claim to be Christians, but they don't act, give, sow or support like a Christian. Many won't bring a supply, but how else is it supposed to be possible?

Do you think Coca-Cola won't supply what it asks for? So why do we struggle with that? Perhaps it's because we've become so self-focused that we've made everything about ourselves! We've learned to tune everything to a radio station I like to call WIFM: What's In It For Me? I don't have a message that says all you have to do is speak faith and believe and then God will bless you immediately. This is my message: if the seed will die, it will produce. However, a seed has to die first in order to produce a plant. That is the progression of life and if you want to walk in prosperity, you need to see this and realize that there are opportunities you've missed. Maybe it's not been $15,000, maybe it was $15, but there are opportunities that you've missed because you weren't connected to God's supply.

God does not honor me because I gave $15,000 and somebody else only gave $2. He honors them equally according to the ability He's given each of us. I would give $15,000 (or other number) because He gave me the ability to give that, so that's why I would do it. Some of you have greater abilities to do things, but you won't do it because you think you have other things to do, but that's why you don't have peace, and that's why you're struggling.

You may have all the money you need but in your heart you have no peace. Your mind may be full of thoughts, wondering if God is happy with you, if He's pleased with you, etc. Did you ever stop and think that might be the conviction of the Holy Ghost trying to draw you near and not away? Did you ever stop and think that this lesson I'm trying to share with you right now could possibly be from the Holy Ghost?

See, there's a war in this world for souls and lives. It's going on outside of the doors of the church building, but how do we ever become effectual if we don't have people that understand how to bring their supply? It does not take much. It only took 12 people to turn the whole world upside down. This isn't an issue of needing more people. If the body of Christ would be more aware of the supply they bring, more would come. If we would realize that if we sow uncommon things and things that cost us, then God will cause us to reap.

You have to tell yourself that God will cause you to reap in the same measure you sow. If you only sow what is comfortable for you, you'll only receive what is comfortable for you. You know you can do better and once you realize that, you will give better.

After that, just see what God does. I can tell you this much: once you figure it out, you'll never want to go back to the way things were. It's hard for me not to think that way now because I've watched how it's all come full circle in my life and in the lives of others. That's just the way I am. Those who know me well know that I will not lie to you. The seeds I planted five or ten years ago, the things I've done to sow seed, are what I lived on when I had nothing. When I say "nothing" I mean *nothing*.

I was being paid $200 a month to pastor, and that was in my second year. The first year, I was pro-bono. Could you live off of $200 a month? Be not deceived, God will not be mocked. That which you sow you shall surely reap (Galatians 6:7). The Amplified says, "That, and only that will you reap." This is the reason people struggle, but it's a very simple answer: how much seed do you have in the ground? How many accounts do you have open right now where you're putting seed in them? I don't mean natural bank accounts, I mean *spiritual* accounts.

Andy Stanley had a quote that has always stuck with me, "Do for one what you wish you could do for everyone." I wish I could be everywhere and in everything, supporting every person, but I can't so there are times in my life where I'll pick somebody and do for one what I wish I could do for everybody. At times, that has kept me in the hospital all night long. There have been times I've given up everything I had when I didn't have much to give. Those are seeds sown.

If I do for everybody and only accomplished a little bit, it would not make as much impact if I were able to find one person and say "I'll do for you what I wish I could do for everybody." I don't know what else to tell you. It's the way it works. I consider those my accounts. As I plant into those accounts, I don't expect them to give me anything in return. I expect God to see what I have done, because He is not unrighteous to forget a labor of love and He always (I mean *always*) brings supply for me. All I have to do is create a need.

TENDING
Engaging Your Faith

1 Corinthians 3:3-9

"For ye are yet carnal: for whereas there is among you envying, and strife, and divisions, are ye not carnal, and walk as men? For while one saith, I am of Paul; and another, I am of Apollos; are ye not carnal? Who then is Paul, and who is Apollos, but ministers by whom ye believed, even as the Lord gave to every man? I have planted, Apollos watered; but God gave the increase. So then neither is he that planteth any thing, neither he that watereth; but God that giveth the increase. Now he that planteth and he that watereth are one: and every man shall receive his own reward according to his own labour. For we are labourers together with God: ye are God's husbandry, ye are God's building."

The word, "husbandry" is Georgian. It's a Greek word that means "A farm or a cultivatable peace of land." The Bible tells you that you are God's husbandry. You are God's field where He plants and receives harvest. You've been designed to produce more and more. He didn't say it's all about Paul who planted the seed or Apollos who watered because neither one of them are more important than God who gave the increase. They operate as one. They bring about what is necessary to put the seed in the ground, but only God can bring increase to the seed.

Anybody can tell you how many seeds are in an apple but only God can tell you how many apples are in the seed. So the seed

39

is something that is designed to produce and God expects you to produce. He does not expect you just to be a receiver and a taker. I call those spiritual vampires; people that come to church, won't tithe, won't serve, won't do anything but show up. All they're doing is sucking the life out of the ministry and they refuse to support and help it. You are not designed just to be a taker, you're designed to be God's husbandry. You're designed to produce fruit and I'm not just talking about financial fruit, I'm talking about fruit, period.

There is a necessity for us to produce the fruit of the Spirit; to be fruitful is a requirement by God not an option. So when you look at your life there should be fruit. Jesus told us that the way we know someone is His disciple is by their fruit. Sometimes, you may see at a nice-looking tree, but that tree may not produce any fruit. If the tree does not produce then we have a problem don't we? What's the purpose of a fruit tree that does not produce fruit? That's why when Jesus went to the fig tree, He cursed it; because it was a hypocrite. Fig trees are not colorful like other fruit trees because the fig fruit grows underneath the leaves.

He went to the tree, looking for the fruit because He saw all of its leaves, but what He saw was an exterior. It appeared to have fruit but when He dug a little deeper, there was none. That's why He cursed it. It wasn't just because He was hungry and angry. He wasn't mad at the tree even though it looked like it was supposed to have fruit, but this is a great understanding of hypocrisy. You can put on the sharp suit, wear a great tie, have your clothes pressed crisp and clean, but if you have no fruit then what's the point? We are expected to produce fruit.

The question is, are you willing to be God's husbandry? Are you really God's building where He is constructing things in your life? Unless the Lord builds the house, he that builds it labors in vain. When hearing that analogy, many wonder if God builds it, then why do we also have to build. God builds it in the spirit, and your job is to build it in the natural. Your job is to take what God has developed spiritually and construct it in your life in the natural. In other words, He created a blueprint.

When you do any type of major construction you have to have an architect to come design a blueprint. The blueprint then tells you how to construct this building. If we built a dog house we probably wouldn't worry about a blueprint or architect, but if you're going to construct a building where someone will live, work, or sleep then you want somebody to design it correctly. Your life should be designed correctly and God has an ultimate plan and blueprint for your life. It is not subject to your opinion, feelings, or your agreement, it's about His perfect will.

He decided from the foundations of the world; He made your blueprint before you were even a twinkle in your daddy's eye, and it does not change because you do or do not like it. It is your job to seek it out. You can build in the natural when your plan lines up with God's because there is always success in God's plan. That's why the scripture said, "Unless the Lord built the house you labor in vain." Most people will decide what they like, what feels good to them and they'll construct that. The sad part is that God didn't design that so when the winds come, it is not built to proper specifications and will not stand.

You are God's husbandry, His building. He is the chief architect and He wants to produce in your life. Many people struggle with this concept in the area of prosperity. Naturally, I don't agree with the idea that all you have to do is say it and you'll have it, but I do believe this: If you are speaking the promises of God and all the promises of God are yes and amen, then if you are lined up with the Word, you are in faith because faith can only be revealed where the will of God is known. If you know that what asking for is in the will of God, then glory to God the answer is yes and amen. Does this mean everybody is going to be a multimillionaire? No. Some of you could not handle it; you'd lose your minds. You'd worship the man-made things, but do I believe we should all be poor? Absolutely not. How do you abound unto every good work as the Bible tells us if we're supposed to be poor? Afterall, the Gospel is the good news and there's no good news in telling me I'm supposed to be broke and struggle with everything in my life. Of course, we'll still have struggles but not everything in your life should be a struggle with no victory in sight. There's a balance to prosperity that comes with responsibility. God is not going to bless you just so you can run around in fancy cars with a fancy house, but He will bless you so you can be a blessing.

Some of you run around saying, "If I had the money I'd give it," but you lie. If you refuse to give a dime when you have it, you're certainly not going to give the dollar either. If you had a million dollars, you're not likely to write a 10% check if you struggle with writing a 10 cent check before. Wait until you start adding some zeros! It's important for you to understand seedtime and harvest because when you sow, if you think that God's going to leave you in a deficit because you sowed into the Kingdom, then your understanding of sacrifice is twisted.

If you think sacrifice means that when you give, you'll never see it again, you are mistaken. If Abraham had thought that way with Isaac, I think he would have had a different understanding and would not have been so quick to obey God. When Isaac asked him what they were going to do he asked where they were going up to worship and where was the sacrifice. Abraham's answer was, "God will provide." He didn't look at him and say, "What do you mean? You! You're the sacrifice." He said God will provide. When you understand sacrifice, what it really means is that what you give to

God means something to you. It does not mean that you go without as a martyr.

Some people want to be self-deified. "Oh, I gave everything I should have to God, now I can't eat but I'm fasting and I'm going to get through it." What happened to the idea that I know if I give to God, He said He's going to take care of me? David said, "I'm old and I was young but I've never seen the righteous forsaken or their seed begging for bread." He's in the Old Testament, so how much more do we have a better covenant built on better promises now? We are able to stand before God and know that as we plant seed, if we are truly His farm, then He will produce in us because He's the one who brings increase.

Paul said, "I planted, Apollos watered but God brought the increase." Some of you have done things for people, expecting them to pay you back. That's why you don't have a harvest. I understand that I am God's farm. So whatever I sow, He will produce the blessing in me. If you think the blessing is coming back from the person you did something for, you will wait for them to do something to bring you increase but they can't bring it to you. However, God said He's the one that bringeth increase regardless of whether they like you, return your phone calls, or ever speak to you again. If you did something and sowed it because God asked you to do it, then it is by His design and His construction, so He will always bring it to pass. Not in them, but in you.

When we understand seedtime and harvest, the Bible says as long as the earth shall remain there's seedtime and harvest. There are seeds of faithfulness that people are sowing today that they will reap later. I served and sowed seeds of faithfulness and now I see those seeds coming to pass. If you understand seedtime and harvest you'll understand everything concerning God because everything comes from seedtime and harvest.

God sowed His son Jesus; one son so that He could have one seed. He said that unless that seed dies, the harvest does not come.

You have to recognize that it is God who brings increase. We work for a living and put all our faith in the job. Then if the job goes under, we lose our minds because we've been laid off or fired. If you're not going through this, you probably know somebody who is. Why are we so moved by the source in our heads but in reality the source is God? Unless you received an e-mail that said God fell off the throne and Jesus is no longer reigning and ruling, there is absolutely no reason to freak out because the blessing is not on the company but on you. Who's His farm? You are; the blessing's on you.

I, Gene, am absolutely nothing. The Christ *in* me is the hope of glory and the anointing. He is the one who opens doors that no man can open and closes doors that no man can close. He is the one who prospers me, the one who leads and guides me into every successful venture and if I listen to His voice and follow His plan, I'll be successful. I do not have to be propped up, but whether or not we understand that, the blessing is not upon the stuff, it's upon you. Regardless of what happens in the world, when you sow generosity you receive generosity. When you sow friendship, you receive friendship. When you sow kindness, you receive kindness.

One of my personal goals is to be a person that can always bring a supply. I don't care what you need or how you need it, I want to bring a supply to help you accomplish what you want in your life. Why do I want to do that? I understand that if I sow that, I will reap similarly in my own life and help you do the same in yours.

See, the challenge is that all some Christian adults sow is strife, contention, discord, their personal opinions, and their feelings. So what do they receive? More strife, contention, and discord because the Bible says "be not deceived, God is not mocked that which you sow you shall reap." Many of the people who do this are disappointed with the life they're living right now, but it's because the seeds have come home to roost. They sowed it even though they don't want to believe they did. They could have sown better seeds but they didn't. They should have, but they didn't.

We are creatures of connection. We often have to see that if you do part A, then part B happens. So if there's a time delay between A and B, it's easy to think there may not be any part B this time. This is how people travel off into places they shouldn't be, then years later these things comes home to roost. This is because of seedtime and harvest. God gave us a very clear understanding of these concepts by using this agricultural analogy. We can clearly understand that if you want corn, you must plant corn. You'd be crazy to plant a bunch of cotton crops and then be mad when cotton grows. It's insane. If you wanted beans, you wouldn't plant corn. Whatever it is you want, you have to plant that because the moment you plant it, that is the seed that is going into the ground and now God will cause the increase.

Mark 4:14-15

"The sower soweth the word. And these are they by the way side, where the word is sown; but when they have heard, Satan cometh immediately, and taketh away the word that was sown in their hearts."

Satan comes immediately to steal from you. If you read in Genesis 15 where Abraham was preparing to cut covenant with God, it says as he laid out the pieces of the animals, the birds of the away. The Bible refers to Satan as a bird of the air who comes to steal from us. The reality is that Satan always comes immediately to disrupt what God is doing in your life. As you move into faith about your seed, gain understanding how to live in a prosperous way and realize that seed is necessary, when you plant your seed Satan will come immediately to try and steal it because if he can, it'll never produce.

If Satan can't take it from you now, through the process of pressure he'll cause you to back away from that seed and he'll steal the harvest. You may say, "I'm in faith. I'm holding fast to it. Father I thank you that my needs are met; I planted that seed." Then, months later when the pressure is greater, your confession changes to, "Man I shouldn't have gave that, that was stupid." You just experienced a drive-by. Satan comes immediately to take it but if he can't take it immediately he will continue to apply pressure. This is why you have to maintain a correct confession because you will have what you say. If you want to say you're sick, you'll have it. If you want to say you're broke, you'll have it. You will have exactly what you say.

That's why you should be very careful what you speak over your children. Be very careful what you speak over your family. Your words are powerful, but Satan comes immediately everywhere the Word is sow to steal it. That's what he does; the thief cometh to steal, kill and destroy. However, Jesus said, "I have come that you may have life to the full, 'til it overflows" (John 10:10). If I have life that overflows, life to the full, if that's what Jesus came to do for me, then He didn't come to keep me in bondage, in fear, or in lack. Why would He have to give His life to leave me in the condition I was in before He gave His life?

There must be something that I am to expect when I say that I'm a Christian. You want to know what it is? You are God's farm, you are His piece of dirt that He plants into and gives increase. All you have to do is become that conduit. I understood a long time ago I could never out-give God. You will never be able to out-give God. I was very young and now I'm not old, but I have never seen the righteous forsaken nor their seed (not other people's seed) begging for bread. I guarantee you, 20-40 years from now I'll be able to say, "I was young, now I'm old," and I guarantee you I will still tell you I've never seen the righteous forsaken.

It's a challenge to our faith because when you don't have faith, it's hard for you to believe, trust, adhere to and rely upon God. It's hard for you when you don't have faith. When you are in the midst of the situation, you need safe people around that you can trust; people that won't fall to pieces every time something goes wrong. "I want to get out of ministry! I want to get out of this," and they're on the other line, "Me too! We should quit together!" No, you need people that, in your moment of weakness, will say, "You'd better pull yourself together! Greater is He that is in you than he that is in the world! We are overcomers, we're going to do this thing. Do I have to come to your house?"

Those are the people that will speak strength into your life and help you gain the proper perspective. Pressure will always come and Satan brings it immediately. Isn't that amazing how he is not slacking? If you want to see laziness, go to the church. The moment Satan thinks you're in faith about something, there he is with an attack. He's not sleeping, not resting, and not slowing down. "Pastor, I'm just taking a break from all this faith stuff." Are you kidding me? I walk by faith, I talk by faith. I breathe by faith. I live by faith. I have no way to function without faith!

Without faith it's impossible to please God. I don't ever take a break from my faith! It is constantly employed in the things I'm believing God for because I'm expecting big things, and how do you have big things without big faith? It's just not possible. I don't have the luxury to be tired because I'm His farm. I want to be the farm that when people drive by, they're like, "Man that's a big farm. There's a lot going on over there!" I understand that I'm His husbandry and that seedtime and harvest is the prevailing law of the kingdom. I understand that if I want, I had better sow.

Mark 4:17

"And have no root in themselves, and so endure but for a time: afterward, when affliction or persecution ariseth for the word's sake, immediately they are offended."

Notice the pattern here? When you build your faith about something— sowing the Word on it, believing the Word, doing the Word— immediately Satan comes to try and steal it. If he can't steal it then he brings persecution and attack, not because of you but because of the Word you're believing in. The moment you start believing more in him than the Word, he has stolen exactly what you planted, and then you're offended.

At this point, many people start thinking, "How come God didn't do this for me?" If that's your question, I have one for you: What do you mean *God didn't do it*? How come *you* didn't stay in faith? How come every time Satan threw something at you, you didn't respond saying, "I shall overcome by the blood of the lamb and the word of my testimony?" Or how about, "I'm going to speak it and know that this is going to happen?" Or even, "God has called me, therefore I am his husbandry and it shall produce. It may not produce when I want it, but I refuse to let Satan have one seed. Everything that God has told me to do, I want to do."

There are things God has put in your heart. It's a desire of yours, but you've allowed yourself to think it's too ridiculous or that it will never happen for you. Thoughts like those are lies from

Satan. It is your responsibility to understand and believe God has revealed these desires and things in your heart by His Spirit. I hear people say things like, "I know one day God's going to use me to finance the kingdom." Unfortunately, for those who refuse to give a nickel, why would God use that person to do something they have not done? If that's what God's really going to do for you then you'll finance it now. You might not finance the whole kingdom, you might finance a couple chairs, but you get in where you fit in and it allows you to watch God increase you and bring you to greater degrees of understanding, revelation, and light.

As you walk in light, you qualify for more light. In my own life, it was hard to believe God for one business. Then when He gave me three and I started to teach Bible college two nights a week and served three nights a week, don't you think somewhere along the line I said, "Oh my God, really?" Guess what? My God shall supply all my needs according to His riches that sit in His bank account. Therefore, I understand that if I'm submitted to His perfect will then there's always provision for the vision! If I'm doing what He's asked me to do, He does not leave me sitting at the table to pay the check. He does not run out and say, "You've got to wash dishes tonight because I don't have the money." If He took you to dinner, He's going to pay for it because that is the God we serve.

He is greater than anything you could ever think, imagine, or believe. There exists this poverty-populated gospel that seems to come from experience. It comes from people who say they were believing God for something and it didn't happen, like God's just going to re-write the Bible because of their experience. This is why I don't preach my experience. I've seen God do things that make no sense whatsoever but if I can't find it in the Word, we'll talk about it when I get to Heaven. Until then, if the Word says He's a healer,

I don't care if I struggle all my life; if the Bible says He's a healer then He's a healer.

I knew a minister who really did struggle most of his ministerial career with sickness. He eventually died of natural causes, not the sickness. Some people were concerned and they were asking, "How come he didn't get healed?" One of the ministers that I follow said, "What makes you think he wasn't? How do you think he stayed in the ministry for as long as he did?" Sometimes your miracle comes to sustain you. You might not be healed of it, but you might be able to function with it like no one else could ever function. Some people wonder why he eventually died. For those who are saved, death is the ultimate healing. We're selfish because we still want them to be in pain on Earth so we can appease our feelings, but we don't realize that God, who has the eternal plan and knows the beginning from the end, knows exactly what's going on and what's about to happen; He's crystal clear on it. In His divine wisdom He decides the right time. We don't know why He made that decision, we don't know what situation was avoided by Him making that decision. All we think about is how much we want what we want.

God architects a plan in the realm of the spirit and one of those plans are for you. He said, "This is what I want for you." Think it not strange that the day you were saved was the day you were saved. Think it not strange that the trouble you go through, there's a reason for that trouble. You have to go through certain things, fight through certain issues and be battle-tested. You cannot stretch your way into Heaven, you have to go through some things because God needs you to increase on this planet so that His plan is perfected.

How can Coca-Cola put a soda on every continent in the world but we can't take the gospel around this world in 2,000 years? They did it in 20 years. Why? Satan is not resisting Coca-Cola, He's not resisting sugar water. He's resisting the living water, he's resisting Christ and he's coming against the plan that God has for you. Why? You are His husbandry and His farm. Be not deceived, God is not mocked. That which you plant you shall reap.

Mark 4:20
"And these are they which are sown on good ground; such as hear the word, and receive it, and bring forth fruit, some thirtyfold, some sixty, and some an hundred."

Luke 8:15
"But that on the good ground are they, which in an honest and good heart, having heard the word, keep it, and bring forth fruit with patience."

Jesus only recognized, in the previous verse, a hundred fold. He does not say some thirty, sixty or a hundred fold. He only says a hundred fold return. You'll hear people say, "If you'll sow into my ministry you'll reap a hundredfold." That is erroneous teaching and it stinks from the pit of Hell. He recognized that if you wanted the hundredfold, He finished with, "Bring forth fruit with patience."

What brings a hundredfold? Patience. Is it the patience of my ministry if you sow into me, or is it your patience? The biblical word "patience" is *hupomeno*, which means "to live under". *Hupo*, like hypoglycemic, and *meno* is "to abide or to live", so patience means to live under. Some of you think biblical patience is you sitting at home doing absolutely nothing while waiting for God to move. Bible patience is to live under the pressure and He said those that stay under and live by faith, they're the ones that are going to receive a hundredfold. If you plant into the ministry, will you receive a harvest? Yes, but whether you receive thirty, sixty or faith. It has to do with your ability to "hupomeno"; to live under the pressure.

So if every time the pressure comes you try to move out from under it, you'd better quit. Under pressure is where diamonds are created and fruit begins to develop. If you're constantly one of those people that every time there's a problem you just want to move out from under the pressure, you will never produce the hundredfold because the hundredfold will only come to those that will endure and constantly speak the Word, staying in faith saying, "I know my God shall supply. I know that I know it may not look good, it may not feel good, but I know that my God has supplied my need according to Christ Jesus."

None of this is according to me, I have to know it and be unconvinced otherwise. Believing like this might unveil people who say things to you like, "You sure don't look prosperous. Look at your car!" So what? That's subject to change and when I'm driving by honking at you while you're walking then we'll see. I will not be robbed of my faith.

Diamonds must be harvested at the right time and the right timing is based on how long they've been under pressure. If you harvest a diamond too soon, all you end up with is a lump of coal. But if you harvest it in its right time, it's the pressure that creates the diamond. People join the ministry, they start serving and all of a sudden they want to take a break because they feel like they're doing too much. Here's what happens; once they back off, Satan will lift the pressure and they'll mistake that as the peace of God. They'll say, "See? I knew God was okay with this." Not even! Now they're walking around with the peace of God in their minds, but the reality is they backed up from under the pressure and wonder why their hundredfold harvest does not come. To hupomeno is to live under it, it's to abide under the pressure.

I am not seeking to move out from under the pressure because I do not care about the situations that I go through. Like Paul said, I've had lots of money and I've had no money. I've abased and I've abound but one thing is for sure, I still trust in Him. He's never left me once. If you can stay under the pressure, you'll see the hundredfold. If you can't, stay long enough to claim your thirty and work at it. Next thing you know you'll receive your sixty. Then at some point in time when you're able to stand, when all hell is breaking loose against you and you're still standing, when everybody's talking bad about you and you're still standing, when the world's coming to and end around you and you're still standing, at that moment if you don't faint or grow weary, you'll receive the hundredfold.

2 Corinthians 9:6
"But this I say, He which soweth sparingly shall reap also sparingly; and he which soweth bountifully shall reap also bountifully."

Does that now tell me that the way in which I sow or the capacity in which I give is how I reap? Is there any other explanation that could be given to that portion of scripture? We can go down to the concordances to break that down, but we do not need to do that. That's pretty clear, the way in which you sow is the way that you will reap.

2 Corinthians 9:7-10
"Every man according as he purposeth in his heart, so let him give; not grudgingly, or of necessity: for God loveth a cheerful giver. And God is able to make all grace abound toward you; that ye, always having all sufficiency in all things, may abound to every good work: (As it is written, He hath dispersed abroad; he hath given to the poor: his

ness remaineth for ever. Now he that ministereth seed to the sower both minister bread for your food, and multiply your seed sown, and increase the fruits of your righteousness.)"

You might be wondering why you don't have a harvest or why God does not give you seed to plant. It's because you won't sow. You think that the seed you currently have, even if it's not enough, you think that's *your* seed. You don't even realize that the little bit you do have is because God gave it to you. The fact that you are drawing breath on this planet is a gift from God. Everything that you have in your life is a gift from God. The fact you are reading this right now is a gift from God.

2 Corinthians 9:10-12

"Now he that ministereth seed to the sower both minister bread for your food, and multiply your seed sown, and increase the fruits of your righteousness;) Being enriched in every thing to all bountifulness, which causeth through us thanksgiving to God. For the administration of this service not only supplieth the want of the saints, but is abundant also by many thanksgivings unto God."

As you give and plant seed into the ministry, you take care of the saints. Since the saints are abundantly supplied, it causes thanksgiving to God because who else would have brought the abundant supply but God? Let's say I take wheat grains and grind them into flour. Then I mix it with other ingredients, maybe some eggs, baking powder, and milk and I make dough out of it. Then I knead the dough, put it in the oven, bake it, and then I have a loaf of bread. Now I've gone through a process that could take me hours, and it all started with the seed.

Some of you eat your seed because you need bread. You eat your seed for nourishment even though God said that if you would sow it He will give you bread for your eating and will multiply the seed you sowed. That means that if I would sow it then God would meet my need. Can we come up with any other interpretation of that? Supernaturally what God is telling you is that He'll give you the thing that you keep your seed for so that you don't have to grind it out, let it rise, knead it out, mix it up. You do not have to do all of that to eat the bread.

Remember, Amos said there comes a time where the one who treadeth out the grapes would overtake the one who planted it (Amos 9:13). In other words, there will come times in the latter rain where you'll be able to sow and reap, and sometimes reap before you even sow because God will supernaturally take your seed and give you bread for your eating and multiply the seed that you've sown.

I learned that if I would just sow the seed, then God said He would give me bread for my eating. He would take care of me. The birds of the air don't sow or plant, yet He still provides. The lilies don't do it, yet Jesus said there reigned one greater than Solomon (Matthew 12:42). See there's a trust, a faith, a reliance, an adherence that has to be placed on God and when you do He said He will give you the bread for your eating and on top of that all the seed you sowed will be multiplied.

I love addition, I love it. Addition is great, but multiplication is awesome. How do you get multiplication? By your obedience, sowing into good soil, and constructing what God told you to construct. You can sow until your fingers fall off but if you are not doing what God asked you to do, you might as well give it up. How faithful is the person that's consciously building what God has asked them to do? Think of how much more they will walk in and abound when they start planting seed and God says, "You know what? You don't have to do all that kneading and rising. You what? You don't have to do all that kneading and rising. You sow it, I'll give you your bread."

I know that flies in the face of people that want to work for it. Your work and your labor are your construction of that which God has already constructed. That's your effort, that's what you're supposed to be doing, not trying to figure out how to find a bigger, better job with promotions. All of that will come if you stay faithful with what God told you to do. You are trying to stay faithful to man instead of staying faithful to God.

Then there are those in the body of Christ that are so disrespectful towards their job because they think God will bless them anyway. However, they refuse to serve the person and the job as unto God (as the Bible tells us to do). Their performance is terrible, yet they want God to bless it. They're the last one to show up to work and the first one to leave and then they say, "My God shall supply all my need," but they're are not giving Him anything to work with. They're sitting at home waiting for a job to knock on their door.

We have a responsibility to model Christ, to live unto God and construct that which God has put in us. When people won't do it, their money just flies away. It's like putting money in a bag with holes in it because they're not committed to what God has asked them to do.

You have to understand there's always provision for His vision. God will never ask you to construct something for which you are not adequately supplied. It's like Jonah's story; If he went to Nineveh first, he would not have had to buy a ticket on a boat and spend three days in the mouth of a fish (which is about as gross of a place to be as I can think of). He paid for that ticket because he would not go where God told him to go, therefore he price. However, if you will do what God's asked you to do, God will pay the ticket.

How cruel of a God would we serve if He asked you to do something that you could not do? How cruel of a God would we have if the desires He put in your heart, He was not able to bring them to pass? The Bible says that hope deferred makes the heart sick but when it comes, it's like a wellspring of life (Proverbs 13:12). Do you think God would put hopes and dreams in your heart that He wasn't willing to bring to pass? God put it in your heart because He wants to bring it to pass but the person you are today is not capable; the one you'll be tomorrow is. Your goal is to see what your tomorrow looks like and construct it in the natural.

This has been the year of education for me. I have no idea why this was the year that I decided to pursue education. I'm so tired of looking at books, I'm so tired of reading, and studying. I've had all I can stand, I am "Popeyed" out! This is what God required of me to go to the next level. I don't need it today, but He said, "You're going to need it." So I began to construct the plan and though I do not yet know why, I just know that's what He asked me to do. As I've done it, He's provided every step of the way.

I'm not trying to teach you rhetoric or hype, I'm trying to show you that God will prosper you beyond your wildest dreams and imagination, but you must be committed to the work and to the plan that God has. It's not so you can ride around in fancy cars, that's not the plan. However, would God give you a fancy car? He can, and He might, but that's not the plan. That's Him blessing you for your faithfulness and your commitment. Can God prosper you? Of course, and He *will* but He'll prosper you for your faithfulness, not just because you want to be wealthy. So before you go thinking about how cool it would be to have a million bucks, know that God couldn't care less about that. It's not about the money for Him, it's about building in this natural world what He has already foreordained in the realm of the spirit. That's why the biggest problem facing the church today is not sin, it's people being unskilled in the things of God. That's the problem.

Jesus dealt with sin thousands of years ago, it's the people of the church that are so unskillful. We've gotten to a place where we think everything is about us. "If you're not going to tell me what I want to hear, that we're all okay, then I'm going to go to the church that has thousands of people in in and preaches that message because I want to have my ears tickled." I want you to be successful because if I could show you the plan He has for my life, you're in it. Your pieces are fitly joined together with my pieces. As we grow together, we unfold the picture, the thousand piece jig-saw puzzle that God has created and foreordained since the very foundations of the world. That's why I'm adamant about getting you to see God's plan for your life and not only to see it but to walk in it.

REAPING
According to Your Measure

Genesis 8:18-22

"And Noah went forth, and his sons, and his wife, and his sons' wives with him: Every beast, every creeping thing, and every fowl, and whatsoever creepeth upon the earth, after their kinds, went forth out of the ark. And Noah builded an altar unto the Lord; and took of every clean beast, and of every clean fowl, and offered burnt offerings on the altar. And the Lord smelled a sweet savour; and the Lord said in his heart, I will not again curse the ground any more for man's sake; for the imagination of man's heart is evil from his youth; neither will I again smite any more every thing living, as I have done. While the earth remaineth, seedtime and harvest, and cold and heat, and summer and winter, and day and night shall not cease."

As long as the earth remains there shall be seedtime and harvest. If all the other things still exist then we are able to understand that seedtime and harvest still exist. We now recognize that if while the earth remains there is seedtime and harvest, cold and heat, summer and winter, day and night; we know that is the principle by which God has reestablished.

When God flooded the Earth He rid the Earth of evil. We understand He promised He would never do that again. That's what a rainbow symbolizes. The sign of a rainbow is God's way of telling us He will never flood the Earth again, despite what the world wants to change the rainbow into and make it a symbol of.

derstand, Christian-wise, what a rainbow is supposed to mean. Despite the perversions that tend to follow that particular symbol, it is not a symbol of sexuality. He said that from that point forward, as long as the earth remains there will be seedtime and harvest time.

People believe prayer will bring a harvest, but prayer does not bring harvest; seed brings harvest. Worry does not bring harvest, nor do good intentions. It's so difficult to teach people about seedtime and harvest because when you hear this message people will argue, "Yeah, well but God knows my heart." God knowing your heart still does not produce harvest.

If you could see tithing and giving from my perspective, you would see that the ones who struggle with their finances are the ones who give the least. I don't mean dollar-wise because some people have more than others, I mean period. You have to give at your level, whatever that level is. When people come to me and say, "Pastor, could you pray for my finances?" The first thing I ask is, "Do you tithe?" If the answer is no, there's nothing left to talk about because what you're asking me to do is witchcraft, which I do not practice.

I do not have a boiling cauldron with frog legs and the eye of a newt. I understand there's seedtime and there's harvest time, and as long as the earth shall remain, seedtime and harvest is the system in which God has setup on how the kingdom functions and operates. When the Bible says, "Be not deceived God is not mocked. That which you sow you shall reap," guess what He's saying. I don't think we have to take out a thesaurus, a dictionary and concordance, and study it in the Hebrew, Greek, or Vines and break it down exponentially.

already put it in His word then that is the truth. Sometimes we have a hard time with that. We want to believe that God will make an exception for us, but it's a lie straight out of the pit of Hell. Crying does not change the Word of God. If lack moved God's hand, then we would not see poverty anywhere. You would not see third-world countries struggling if just the mere sight of lack and the desire to prosper would move God's hand. So there must be something more beyond worry, fear and just "praying it through."

I'm not discounting prayer, but some people have a false impression that prayer will move God's hand. Prayer does not move God's hand; prayer positions you to receive what God has *already* done. If you don't believe me then tell me why Buddhists pray, Hindus pray, and Islamists pray. Prayer in and of itself means absolutely nothing if you are not praying to the God of Abraham, Isaac and Jacob. Prayer in and of itself does not reveal anything unless you know what you already have.

That's why it says those who come to God must come to Him and know that He is. How do you know that He is? You'd better know His Word. If you know His Word then you'll know He's a miracle worker. It's hard to convince me that God can't produce miracles because I have too much Word in me. I know the Word and I know what the Word says. The Word itself is anointed, His Word, He said, will not return void but that He hovers over His Word and He hastens to perform it (Isaiah 55:11). He hovers over His Word looking for an opportunity to bring His Word into reality.

When you are speaking the Word of God in your situation if you don't know the Word and you speak Satan's word, Satan hovers to hasten to perform his word because he's an imitator. God said He's hovering to perform His Word, looking for an opportunity to bring it to pass in your life. It has to be His word, not yours. Not the expression of your fear, worry, hurt or tried tithing one time and it didn't work." If you say you *tried* something and it did not work, it was *not* on God's end! There is no way that I'll allow anybody to tell me that God failed them. I'm just not willing to do it.

When we understand who God really is then it's very easy for you to know that if you can't find it in His Word, you will not find it in Him. He and His Word are one in the same. I love people, I'm not trying to make light of struggles, but if you don't understand seedtime and harvest you will never prosper the way God wants you to. You can worry until your head falls off and cry until you have no more tears left, but you will not move the hand of God. If you want to move the hand of God then you have to have faith. Faith is an expectation that God will do exactly what He told you He will do but you can't have that unless you know what the will of God is.

The will of God is not revealed by anywhere other than His Word. When you understand His Word concerning you then you realize if He said seedtime is what produces harvest time, then you better have seed. You can't eat or store your seed, you have to sow seed. You must be a sower and a giver to walk in God's prosperity. If you are not a giver, if you are very stingy, if you have every reason in the world why you cannot give to God, you will never walk in what God has for you. It's not my opinion, it's a statement of fact.

2 Corinthians 9:6
"But this I say, He which soweth sparingly shall reap also sparingly; and he which soweth bountifully shall reap also bountifully."

Whatever your ability is, that's how you give. In other words if you make $5 a week, God does not expect you to give $5 a week, He expects you to give 50 cents. If you make $5,000 a week then God expects you to give, at minimum, $500 a week. You give according to the several ability of the individual who is giving. It's not about a numerical value. If you think I'm preaching money out of your pocket, I couldn't care less. You are not my source, you never have been my source, you never will be my source.

My source is God. If every person in the church stopped giving, He will move Heaven and Hell to bless me because of my commitment and the seeds I've sown. So I'm not worried about that, just so I can be clear. Sometimes when people hear you talk about this subject Satan will throw things at them. "The only reason why he's talking about this is so he can do...." No, I'm talking about this is so that *you* can be blessed.

In the church I came up in, people always wanted to work for me because they knew I was prosperous and when I would tell them what it took they'd say things like, "Well, can't I just come work for you?" No, my prosperity is for me because of seeds I've sown. However, if you want to come work as hard as I work and do what I do then God will bless you. He's no respecter of persons, but it is amazing how many people did not want to do that. What they wanted was to catch the low-hanging fruit off of my tree. So you must understand that it is *your* responsibility to plant seed. It's *your* responsibility to sow and He said that for those that give sparingly, you receive sparingly.

We know that if we sow one, we only receive one. If you are living in a place where you're constantly wondering where your provision is, then you have to stop and ask yourself, "If I only got one, then that means on the other side of this thing..." People don't make that connection though and then they live in lack, upset with

God because they've "prayed it through." You can call everybody you know and form a prayer line, but if you have not planted any seed, what are you looking for?

I'm Joe Farmer; I walk outside, I see hundreds of acres and I'm mad. There is no corn! So then somebody walks up beside Joe Farmer and says, "What are you mad about?"
"There ain't no corn out there!"
"Well, how much corn did you plant?"
"I didn't plant any."

You immediately say, "Dumb farmer!" So why don't we think that way when it comes to our own prosperity? Why are we looking at empty fields expecting harvest from seed that we didn't sow? He said those that give sparingly reap sparingly and those that give bountifully reap bountifully. Notice He says something; don't let them give grudgingly but as they purpose in their heart. Not out of necessity, not grudgingly but as you purpose in your heart to give.

It's funny because notice the first thing he said was, "Every man according to how he purposed in his heart." If you don't have a heart revelation of seedtime and harvest, you can give out of obedience per say, or because you heard me preach that you should give, but you need to know down into your spirit and in your heart that if you sow you shall surely reap and that which you sow you shall reap. God will make every seed produce and perform according to the nature of the seed that you've sown and if you keep yourself in faith, then that seed will have to produce and it will produce for you. After it is in your heart, then you give.

Here's what I know: I watch people that tithe and they do it because they saw Jimmy do it. They do it because they're tired of hearing my mouth say it to them but it's really not in their heart. If then God will never leave you because that's the essence of faith. It's the place of trust where you say, "I know that God won't leave me. I know He'll always deliver and if I know that then every time I put out seed there's a harvest; some thirty, some sixty, some a hundredfold. It's according to my faith. Whether I get a thirtyfold return, a sixtyfold or a hundredfold is not according to anybody but me."

I remember one time T.D. Jakes said that people pray and pray, and they want a tree, and they get ticked off when God drops an acorn. "I want an oak tree, God!" And God gives you an acorn. Why does God give you an acorn? It's very clear, it is about seed. If I asked you how long a piece of string was, is there a specific answer for that? If you ask me for a tree and I give you an acorn, what am I telling you? I'm giving you a tree and the size of that tree, how long your piece of string will be will be dependent upon your planting, watering, and tending. The bigger the harvest, the greater the sowing. If you want something from God, you better believe that it always starts with seed.

That's why Jesus said that the Kingdom cannot come unless the seed dies in the ground. His fruit was to bring about the kingdom, he had to die first. The seed is necessary because in the seed produces after its own kind; Genesis tells us that. If I say, "Lord I want a tree." I didn't say the size of the tree. He says, "Well here's a seed because now you can have whatever size tree you want." It will be dependent upon you; how much care you take over your seed, how diligent you are about your seed. It has to be how your purpose in your heart.

You can't have faith based on my revelation. I think Christians would walk in greater degrees of prosperity if they would understand this concept. However, because the world tells you to be cheap and not give, people think it's crazy to give God

I think it's crazy to *not* give God 10% because I want 90%. If I want 90% then I need to put the 10% where it's supposed to go so I can receive 90%. Giving grudgingly or out of necessity is always a revealer that you have not purposed correctly in your heart. When you talk about giving and tithing and people get angry about it, then it's an instant revealer that they don't have the correct purposes in their heart.

2 Corinthians 9:8 continues on to say, "And God is able to make all grace abound toward you." You mean to tell me that if I give, God is able to make all grace abound towards me? We don't read one scripture without the rest of it, and the subject here is giving and getting bountifully. It says if you do that, it will cause God to extend more grace towards you. The reason for the grace towards you is that you always, always, having all sufficiency in all things, may abound to every good work. He said He'll make His grace abound towards you. If you would understand how to invoke the process of seed and harvest, He will make His grace abound towards you so that you would have all sufficiency in all things and be able to abound unto every good work. Would you like to have all sufficiency in all things? Do you know what it means to be sufficient? It's where whatever is required to meet the need is supplied. When someone says, "I'm self sufficient," what does that mean? It means that everything I need, I have. You want to go on vacation? You can go.

I've struggled with something personally and I'm going to share it with you. I felt guilty sometimes because I do not struggle, and I know what it feels like to have struggled, but I honestly felt bad. I don't have those same problems. I see other people struggling with this and that...etc. Facebook is the revealer of hearts of the world. You can observe the pulse of the world through Facebook. I see people creating posts about how they're struggling to see a movie at the theater. Dear God, I don't have that problem!

Whatever I want to do, I can do. It might take a little while to save up, but I do not have the feeling within me that I have to struggle. Every need is supplied, I don't care what it is and I used to ask God, "Am I doing something wrong?" Honestly, I really did struggle with that. I got over it, don't get me wrong, but it's a whole different experience when you don't see everything as an obstacle. If things go wrong and the money is there to fix it, deal with it. It's like walking in an ever-abundant supply.

It's like this: Let's say I'm going to give you a choice between giving you a million dollars or a hundred dollar bill that never runs out. I'm not, but *if* I told you that, if you were smart, you would take the $100 bill that never runs out because in time, it'll be valued for more than a million dollars! Since I understand seedtime and harvest, I feel like God has given me His credit card.

When I was younger, I always tried to have possession of my parents' credit card, and to be honest with you they would never let me borrow their card. If your parents did that for you, you're blessed and you're better than me because they would never give it to me (and I think they knew not to because I had expensive taste). Can you imagine the lifestyle you would live when you were able to say you're using God's credit card? Now, I don't mean that you live sloppily, crazy, reckless, and careless (not being a wise steward). I'm just saying that all my needs are met — all of them and some of my wants.

I don't struggle or labor over it. When the bills are due, the bills are due. Call them up and say, "Here you go." Some of them are now on auto. I never thought I'd get to the day when that happened. There used to be a day where I'd be like, "Look I need you to take that out on the 14th because if you take it out on the 15th you're going to mess up my other bills." You know how it is.

want you to understand that I understand, but I don't live like that anymore. It doesn't matter what day, my God supplies all of my needs.

How did I get to that place? I understood seedtime and harvest. Seed is everything; that which you sow you shall surely reap. He said if you give bountifully, God will make all grace abound towards you. Not towards anything else, but to you that you'll have all sufficiency. Then He goes on to say in 2 Corinthians 9:9-10, "*He hath dispersed abroad; he hath given to the poor: his righteousness remaineth for ever. Now he that ministereth seed to the sower both minister bread for your food, and multiply your seed sown, and increase the fruits of your righteousness.)*" So He gives bread to the sower and seed to the sower. That means that if you're not a sower, you don't qualify. I don't care how much you pray, I don't care how much you beg.

"Now he that ministers seed to the sower..." not the one who says, "Well, you know Lord, I'm working on it. I'm going to get there. I'm just planning on it." He gives seed to the sower. Not to the eater, not to the hoarder, but to the sower. When He knows that He can get it *through* you then He's more willing to get it *to* you. If He cannot get it through you because you have to stop and nibble on what does not belong to you, that's another story.

See, some of you struggle with giving because you think your money is *your* money. You give no glory to God, you don't even think the fact that you're drawing breath right now is a gift that God gave you. You don't even think that the job you have (or don't have) God gave you. Whatever it is that you desire, anything in your life, is dependent upon God. It's self-deification.

We're in a society where people have deified themselves into God. They feel that they can re-define what marriage is, they can re-define what is right and wrong, redefine genders, or anything they want to because they've decided they're God. Well, I can tell you what; there will come a moment and a time where the trumpets will sound and we will rise. In that moment there will no longer be a choice between what is right and what is wrong. It will be a sad state of affairs for all those who deified themselves and neglected the one true God. I learned a long time ago that it is but by the grace of God that anything is going well.

I'm looking to offend your mind to reveal your heart to you. The realities are the Word of God is offensive. I don't know why people think it's not. "Oh you know I don't get offended by the Word." You're not reading it. "Well, Jesus wasn't offensive." You have not listened to anything Jesus said if you think that. If you had, you would know He did not come to play at all, not even a little bit.

Romans 12:1-6
"I beseech you therefore, brethren, by the mercies of God, that ye present your bodies a living sacrifice, holy, acceptable unto God, which is your reasonable service. And be not conformed to this world: but be ye transformed by the renewing of your mind, that ye may prove what is that good, and acceptable, and perfect, will of God. For I say, through the grace given unto me, to every man that is among you, not to think of himself more highly than he ought to think; but to think soberly, according as God hath dealt to every man the measure of faith. For as we have many members in one body, and all members have not the same office: So we, being many, are one body in Christ, and every one members one of another. Having then gifts differing according to the grace that is given to us, whether prophecy, let us prophesy according to the proportion of faith."

He said, "I have been given grace and I understand the supply or the measure of faith that I've been given to walk in that grace." He goes on to say the body has different parts with different functions. "So is the body of Christ." That means there is a grace given to you that is not on someone else and it's based on their part as they fit into the body. He said not to think of yourself more highly than you should.

Let's say somebody's the armpit. You don't have the right to be boastful. "Yeah! I'm the armpit and I'm going to tell everybody what to do and boss this whole thing around!" Somebody's going to look at you and say, "You kind of stink a little bit." You're the armpit, stay in your lane. Maybe I'm the ears. So if I over inflate my importance as the ears then what do we do about our sight? Have you ever noticed that those who lose a particular sense will heighten other senses? If they go blind they can hear a pin drop. The body will naturally compensate for what is missing, but when all the parts are functioning together properly no one part has to work extra hard.

He said every part should not think more highly of itself than it ought. Basically, stay in your lane and do what it is God has graced you to do. That's why you'd best be careful. I need the grace that's in every one of you because you have a supply. It's just as you fit as a part of the body and we all have gifts that are differing according to the grace that God has given you, and the measure of faith to walk in that grace. Whatever you can do, God gave you the gift of faith to walk in what He called you to do.

According to His grace He also gave you the measure of the grace you need to be the eyes, ears, or whatever part you are in the body. "Having then gifts differing according to the grace that is given to us, whether prophecy, let us prophesy according to the proportion of faith." That's not referring to God's faith. So if you have the gift of prophecy, prophesy according to the portion of faith that *you* have.

Now, some people think they're a prophet when they really have the *gift* of prophesy. Some people think they're an evangelist when they have the gift of exhortation. "Or ministry, let us wait on our ministering: or he that teacheth, on teaching; Or he that exhorteth, on exhortation: he that giveth, let him do it with simplicity; he that ruleth, with diligence; he that sheweth mercy, with cheerfulness." (Romans 12:7-8) Paul is outlining the ministry gifts that have been placed in the body. He that has prophecy, let him prophesy according to the proportion of faith that they have. If you're an exhorter, exhort.

However, there is a problem. There are a lot of people that have the gift of exhortation and they're in the evangelistic office thinking, "I can preach the paint off the walls." Just because you can preach, that does not make you a pastor, an evangelist or a prophet. There are office requirements that come with those gifts as God has placed them in the body for a particular function.

Maybe you can preach the paint off the walls, but all your sheep are sick. They're walking around talking about how broke they are, "Well one day God will heal me…" but you can preach the paint off the walls. Unless they can eat the paint that falls off the walls, how is that helping anybody? There are differing gifts that come with the responsibility that is placed in every gift God has given. Just because they exhort does not mean they're ready for the office, it's a gift. Prophecy is a gift.

Why is it that everybody can recognize when they want to *prophe-lie*? (Notice, this does not mean prophesy, this is a prophe-lie). Why can they recognize that gift? They come and tell you, "Oh I've been given the gift to teach." until you say, "Go kids." Then they don't want to teach anymore. "I've been given a gift to exhort. Pastor, when can I get up and preach from the pulpit? I just got the fire!" No you don't, sit down. Yet, the next verse in 2 Corinthians 9 says, "For he that giveth let him do it with simplicity." You mean to tell me that there's a grace that God will give to someone for them to give? That some people are graced with that?

Here's what I knew; I'm going to share something with you. I made the decision years ago, probably 13 years ago, that I was going to be a distribution center for God. I was going to be a conduit by which it came through me. After I made that decision, I now have 3-4 businesses making boatloads of money because I understood there was a grace that came with giving. If I walked in that then I knew according to my measure of faith I could walk in that gift. God gave me a measure of faith to walk in that grace. Do you ever hear people say, "I was called to the kids area but the grace lifted on that so God moved me on," or something similar? That means they stepped out of faith. We access grace by faith, so if you think the grace has lifted what actually happened was you stopped using your faith and now you cannot access the grace.

I was in Pawnee, Oklahoma with my spiritual father and he asked me to receive the offering. The Lord had given me something, that there were people in that room that had purposed in their heart to connect with his ministry and really give sacrificially to see the gospel flow through that ministry. So when I got up, I started talking about that. It was so quiet in there — I mean *quiet*! I thought, "Maybe I missed it." So when I was done, we received the offering. I had four different businessmen in his church come up to me afterwards and told me, "God spoke to me personally years ago and told me to do that; to connect to his ministry, to sow into it sacrificially and God told me He would prosper me. I was just afraid to do it."

You know, I'm glad that they came and told me that because it helped me to know that I didn't miss it. It also saddened me at the same time because I thought to myself, "Where would you have been today if you had have moved when God told you to move; if you had have sown when God told you to sow?" There's a grace for it. Grace is unmerited favor. It takes you beyond who you really are today.

Some of you are living in mercy, just barely managing yourself and you say, "God's supplying." No He's not; that's mercy. Mercy is when you can pay your own bills, grace is when you can start paying other people's bills. There's a difference; barely getting by versus more than enough.

God moved His people through the wilderness and took them out of Egypt, which was lack. He took them *into* the wilderness, which was barely enough. "Give us this day our daily bread." Where does that come from? Daily manna. God provided daily. That was just enough, but He was moving them into the place of more than enough. The land of Canaan was an abundant supply. God took them from lack, to just enough, to more than enough. It took them 40 years to get there because they thought like lack instead of moving into prosperity.

You can't be an Egyptian *and* walk in abundance. You know how they say that you can take the brother out of the hood but you can't take the hood out of the brother? You can take people out of Egypt but it's hard to take the Egypt out of them. When you understand this you will see things differently.

When you look at money, you either look at it one of two ways; you are either going to spend it or you're going to invest it. I don't spend money, I rarely spend money, I invest it. When you look at your time, you can look at it two ways; you can either spend it or invest it. I don't spend time, I hate spending time. I don't like anyone that much to just want to spend time, I *invest* time. If people want access to me, they must demonstrate that they understand when I spend the time it's an investment. It's not just hanging out. You don't know me, you know my gift so that's what I invest.

When you look at your finances, do you really think to yourself, "I should invest this," then do it? How do you invest it? Paul said he prayed that our finances will abound unto our heavenly account where moth do not eat and rust does not erode. So when you give into the work that God has put you in, into that ministry, you're not sowing to the pastor or the church, you're really sowing to God. When you give unto God, the Bible tells you that everything you gave gets converted into your heavenly account.

Everything that you spend burns up like wood, hay and stubble. However, everything you sow into the Kingdom will abound unto your heavenly account. So if you get to Heaven and there's nothing in your account, then you will unfortunately realize where you missed it. The problem is it's too late then. I'm trying to help you to the best of my ability because I want you to understand as long as the earth remains there will be seedtime and harvest time. Your "shoulda-coulda-woulda's" don't move God. You don't think He's heard all that before?

Romans 12:8-11
"Or he that exhorteth, on exhortation: he that giveth, let him do it with simplicity; he that ruleth, with diligence; he that sheweth mercy, with cheerfulness. Let love be without dissimulation. Abhor that which is evil; cleave to that which is good. Be kindly affectioned one to another with brotherly

It is amazing that he begins to lay out all the administrative gifts in the church. One of those gifts is the gift of giving and he says it's in every body. In every body there are those that have been graced to give. How do you know you've been graced with it? You seem to have a desire to want to fund the Kingdom. That's how you know because the faith is there, that's why you think that way.

Some of you get stuck in that place of, "Man if I just had it I would fund the kingdom. I would do big things!" You'd better do big things before you have big things because you doing the big things now is the sign of your faith of the big things to come. He said, "And when you do that bountifully then will I make all grace abound towards you to empower you to do what it is in your heart you believe you should do." If it's not in your heart, you missed it.

Genesis 3:16
"Unto the woman he said, I will greatly multiply thy sorrow and thy conception; in sorrow thou shalt bring forth children; and thy desire shall be to thy husband, and he shall rule over thee. And unto Adam he said, Because thou hast hearkened unto the voice of thy wife, and hast eaten of the tree, of which I commanded thee, saying, Thou shalt not eat of it: cursed is the ground for thy sake; in sorrow shalt thou eat of it all the days of thy life."

Proverbs 10:22
"The blessing of the Lord, it maketh rich, and he addeth no sorrow with it."

God cursed the ground because of man. The ground cannot produce a full harvest. If I plant one I should get one. In God's terms, there's multiplication involved. If I plant one I can reap sixty, thirty or a hundred. However, if the ground is cursed, now when I plant one I may only get one. He said, "In sorrow." What does sorrow mean? Effort, toil, real strong labor. You have to work really hard. So the curse that was on the ground caused Him to tell Adam, "You are going to eat of this land but you're going to work it from the sweat of your brow. You are literally going to kill yourself to make a living." Then He says, "I will no longer curse this ground for man's sake" (Genesis 8:21). That's why it says the blessing of the Lord maketh rich and adds no sorrow, toil or effort.

Can you be lazy and prosper? No. The ground is cursed for the world. It will only produce a little bit for them but for you and I who understand that the curse has been lifted and when God put His blessing upon us, now that's where you get the thirty, sixty and a hundred fold. Then you ask, "If so-and-so walks in here, an unbeliever, and hands in a check for a million dollars and walks out, will they reap a harvest off of that?" As long as the earth shall remain, will they reap a harvest off of that? Will they be blessed because of seed they've sown? Yes, but the one who understands that it's the blessing of the Lord that maketh rich and adds no sorrow to it shall reap even more.

What if a believer comes in the door, a tongue-talking, spirit-filled, Bible-believing believer, hands in a million dollar check and walks out? Should they expect to have more of a return? Yes, because the blessing of the Lord is what maketh rich and adds no sorrow to it. If you have to work for ten companies to make ends meet, you are toiling. You are not walking in the blessing because the sign of the anointing is that you can do more with less. The world will convince you to think you need ten jobs. No, you don't. You need to find ten scriptures and start meditating day and night, murmuring them every chance you get until it is buried so far in you that you realize all you have to do is what God asked you to do and if you do what He's asked you to do, then the blessing of the Lord is what maketh rich, and He adds no sorrow to

Genesis 3:18

"Thorns also and thistles shall it bring forth to thee; and thou shalt eat the herb of the field; In the sweat of thy face shalt thou eat bread, till thou return unto the ground; for out of it wast thou taken: for dust thou art, and unto dust shalt thou return."

Sorrow does not mean he was sad, it means he was sweating and working hard to gain nothing. Who can relate? Working hard to obtain nothing. It's the blessing of the Lord that maketh rich and adds no sweat of your face to it. When you understand seedtime and harvest, when you understand the blessing's on you, then you realize when you show up to work, the blessing just showed up. When you arrive at the car dealership looking for a car, the blessing just showed up. You should expect to receive more than what anybody else received. I don't care if they were doing a deal for Mickey Mouse ten seconds earlier and they gave him the best deal on the planet. When you walk in the door, you should expect to have a better deal.

Things that cause me sorrow have to go. Will I work hard? Of course I will. I'll put in the time, but I'm not going to do it in sorrow. I'm not going to do it being aggravated. I will cut something quick that gets on my nerves. I just don't have the time nor patience. I understand that if I stay focused on my seed and I'm continually putting seed in all the time, then God can multiply my seed sown. However, if I have not planted any seed, if I'm unwilling to tithe, if I have every excuse in the book why I don't do it then I'm going to reap that. Then, you'll have every excuse in the book why you don't have what you're expecting. You can cry until your tear ducts shut down, it does not move God.

There's plenty of lack and poverty all across the world. God's hand is only moved when somebody makes a decision to walk in faith. Remember, Jesus said if you see a miracle done that brings glory to God then you know that the Kingdom of God has just come upon you. How do you know where the Kingdom of God is? When the blessing shows up, the Kingdom of God is upon you.

Next time you go to a job interview you need to let them know, "If you hire me, this thing will grow, guarantee it." When we moved into our first church building, there was nobody else in the whole plaza other than the guy next to us and a clothing store. When we moved in I told the landlord, "If you put us in this place, it'll start filling up," and it did. They started making some bad decisions so they lost some business, but prior to that it started filling up just because we were there. If you understand that the blessing's on you then you know you have favor wherever you go.

You walk into the store, it's not just a 5% off sale, it's a 30% - 50% off sale. You should expect them to bless you because the blessing is on you. As long as the earth remains, there will be seedtime and there will be harvest. How you plant and sow will determine how you reap. If you want to change how you reap, you'd better change how you sow. If you do that, I'm telling you, strap in because you'll be going through the roof. When you do, everybody around you who didn't get it will want to turn towards you and, of course, catch the low-hanging fruit.

It's a principle that is biblical. It's real and it's one of the most violated principles out there. Ministry is all about sowing. If you know you have a call into ministry, you need to sow correctly because when you start your ministry you'll be surrounded by people who act like you. For some of you that's encouragement, for some of you that's condemnation or conviction. Call it whatever you want to call it, but remember; how you sow you shall reap. If sow friendship, you'll reap friendship. If you sow love, you'll get love. If you sow faithfulness, you'll get faithfulness.

I'm aware of how faithful a lot of the people in my church are. Those are seeds I sowed when I followed my pastor and carried his bag for 8-9 years. I served under him and made sure everything he needed was taken care of. Those were seeds that I've sown, but then people want to get in ministry, and they want it all immediately. It does not work like that. You have to put some seed in the ground and nurture it, speak the Word over, it and let it produce in your life. I promise you if you learn this, you will see greater degrees of harvest than you've ever seen before because it's a law.

Is there a law of gravity? Yes. When does the law of gravity work against you? When your elevation has exceeded a reasonable distance by which the law of gravity takes effect. Is the law of gravity in effect right now? Yes. Will it kill you? No, but if you go up about 100 feet and jump, will the law of gravity kill you? Yes.

Laws always work. Whether they work for or against you is based on how much respect you have for it. I can go on top of a building, look out into the city, but I'm not jumping because I have respect for the law of gravity. I may be flying down the highway where the speed limit is 65mph, I might go up to about 70mph. Many have no respect for that law. The law of sowing and reaping whether you like it, whether you agree with it, whether you want to, it is still a law and it will only work for you when you cooperate with it. When you refuse to cooperate with it, it'll work against you.

SUPPLYING
Not Observing The Wind

Genesis 8:22
"While the earth remaineth, seedtime and harvest, and cold and heat, and summer and winter, and day and night shall not cease."

Things from a biblical standpoint always operate on seedtime and harvest time. It likens the Kingdom of God to seedtime and harvest because what you plant is what you reap. The only difference is that if you plant it in God, it will be multiplied and you'll receive more because God will give increase. That's why the Bible says that Paul planted, Apollos watered, but God was the one who brought the increase.

What we don't necessarily understand is that seedtime and harvest governs every biblical principle there is. Everything works off the premise of seed and your harvest. The Bible tells us that while the earth remains, there will always be seedtime and harvest, cold and heat, winter and summer, day and night. In Arizona, sometimes I wish this heat would cease for just a little bit, but the reality is it has not stopped. So then if we are able to say that has not stopped, then we can also say that seedtime and harvest have not ceased.

So when we look at our prosperity do we ever really understand that your prosperity is tied to your seed? Whether you plant seed or whether you don't plant seed, are you a giver or are you not a giver? Are you one that counts everything down to the when you're dealing with God or are you a person who's generous towards the things of God? You have to make some decisions about who you're going to be because I guarantee you the way that you handle God is the way He handles you. That's why he says the way that you sow is the way that you'll reap.

Luke 6:38

"Give, and it shall be given unto you; good measure, pressed down, and shaken together, and running over, shall men give into your bosom. For with the same measure that ye mete withal it shall be measured to you again."

If I told you that I was going to fill either a bucket or an Altoid tin with money and give it to you, which would you prefer? If you are giving like the Altoid tin, you will not reap like the bucket. That's exactly what it just said. The measuring cup, the device you use to measure, how you give, is the measuring stick that is used when men give back unto you. As many times as people have heard this, I don't know if they realize how they give shall be given back to them.

Now, will God provide the increase? Sure, but if you want to see the bucket-full, then you have to give like you have the bucket. Everybody is prospered at a different level, but the point I'm getting at is that the bucket is different for each person. This might be a dollar for some, might be a million dollars for others. It's not necessarily that you have to give like other people give, you just have to do what is generous for *you*.

Then, it says when you give it will be given back unto you, not from God directly but it'll cause you to have favor with men, or people, and they will open doors up for you and pour out blessings into your bosom that literally will be measured by the same measuring stick in which you give. Now like I said, for some that's and for some that's an indictment, but it's still the Word of God. You have to recognize that the measure in which you receive is a spiritual law.

If you were to plant an acre of corn, you should expect to grown an acre of corn. However you plant it is how you'll reap. So the measuring stick by which you give will be the measuring stick by which you receive. So if every time the offering comes around you come in with a little teaspoon, don't be mad when all you get is 5% off when you go to the store. Don't be mad when you don't have tremendous favor and wonder why you don't have favor.

People give my wife and I things for free. All we have to do is show up and talk to them. They'll just bless us and do things for us; they'll hook us up. I have favor. Why do I have favor? I give abundantly and the measure in which I give is the measure that I expect it to come back to me. It is amazing how people want to walk in favor and they're wondering, "Why can't I walk in the blessing? Why is it always so hard for me? Why is everything so difficult?" It's because of how you give.

Now, let's just assume for the sake of this discussion that you are an abundant giver. I love how when I ask the question "Are you a tither?" People say, "Well, sometimes." If it's just "sometimes" then you're not a tither! The definition of a tither is you give 10% of your income to God. If you give it sometimes and not other times you don't give 10%, you give an averaged mean of what you're giving has been but it is not 10%. So therefore if you don't bring your tithe into the storehouse, the Bible says you're cursed with a curse. What do you want us to do? I can't teach something that's outside of the Bible, it's just that simple.

Whether we like it or don't like it, it's the truth. If you're still saying, "Well I do that but I still don't get a return," then you don't expect it. If you are an abundant giver then this is the Scripture that tells you that everywhere you go, He says He will cause men to give unto you in the same way you give unto Him. God will cause people to do it. You know what causing somebody to do something is? God will grab them by their collar and cause them. That means I get to expect and to anticipate that everywhere I go, God has already gone before me and He will cause them to.

I walk in favor. I am surrounded with favor. Everywhere I go I'm surrounded with favor. Do you realize that everywhere you go, *you* are surrounded with favor? Everywhere you go, opportunity should present itself. God said, "I've given you that land." That's what He told Joshua. All you need to do is follow His commandments. Observe to do all that He told you to do; not some, not sometimes, but *all*. If you do that, then everywhere you put your foot you'll find favor.

I *know* that everywhere I go, I expect favor. It's agitating to some people because if they go in my stead, I expect them to know that I expect favor. God promised me that the same measure that I give is how I am to expect it to come back. If your measuring cup is an Altoid tin or a big old trash bin, that's how it comes back to you. If you're only getting a little then I guarantee you it's because you give little.

"Well, I give more than so-and-so." Well, I'm glad you measure yourself among yourselves but the Bible tells us that isn't wise (2 Corinthians 10:12). I don't care how much so-and-so gives, that has nothing to do with me. What I give is based on the revelation God gave me. What you are to give is based on the revelation God gave you, what He expects of you. You have a responsibility to bring a supply to the work of God. Every nickel that this ministry needs, if we want to be honest, it's in your pockets. Every ministry we want to start — the food banks, we want to start — the food banks, outreaches — all the things that we want to do is in your pockets. It's not in mine, it's in yours.

A friend of mine who pastors a church in New York ran a survey. They asked the people where they think the money comes from to do ministry. Do you realize that a majority of the people thought there was a fund out there that takes care of churches? There is a fund somewhere and if this book contained a mirror, here's where I'd tell you to hold it up to yourself. There is a fund that takes care of the church, *it's you*.

Do you think God would be so unrighteous to ask you to support His work without blessing you? Do you think God would ever leave you? Do you think He'd ever forsake you? Why can't we get there in our faith? The number one reason why people don't give is that they're afraid God will not do it this time. They'll go to Starbucks and spend $5 for something that costs $0.10 to produce and they could have made it at home, but because of the convenience and all the wonderful flavors, they'll casually spend it, but when you talk about giving to the ministry, people won't want to hear it.

I remember when gas prices had gone through the roof. By "through the roof" I mean it was priced around $5 per gallon. Everybody was tripping out all over Facebook like the world was coming to an end when gas in Europe is $8 per gallon. Yet (and still) we're freaking out over $5 gas but we certainly don't freak out over $5 Macchiatos, extra whipped, with two pumps of vanilla. It's bizarre. I have an F-250 truck that has two gas tanks on it. When gas was $5 per gallon it cost me $140 to fill that truck up. I didn't think to myself, "I'm so upset about how high gas prices are." All I could think was, "I'm so glad that I'm so blessed that I don't care what gas comes to. If it becomes $10 a gallon my God shall supply all of my need."

It does not matter what it becomes, but boy you should see the people, "Ouch! This is ridiculous!" Thank God that my God will cause men to give unto me in the same measure in which I give it is the same measure in which I expect to receive it. If I am generous towards the things of God, then I know that God is generous towards me so I know that He will always supply my need according to His riches in Christ Jesus. I don't care what gas comes out to be, about inflation, recession, or the economy. I am not subject to that.

I hear preachers say, "Well the economy is bad so I don't want to teach my people about giving because they might be worse off." That's the time you *should* be teaching it because the only thing that holds eternal is the Word of God. The *only thing* that has an anointing on it when all hell is broken loose is the Word of God. If you want to grow, you have to know the Word of God on the matter so that you will prosper when everyone else is failing. The only thing that will make the difference is your understanding of the Word and its application in your life.

I'm not going to sit here and say, "Well I don't want to teach that because God might not answer their prayers." Let me tell you something; God will never leave you nor forsake you. You will never out-give God. I don't care how sacrificial you become, you will never out-give God. I don't care how much or whatever you do. Here's what I do know; the people that have a revelation of tithing and giving, I've watched them grow. That's why I'm so confident in preaching it. If you think I'm preaching money out of your pocket, go give it to another ministry. When it works, take it back to your church, because you should always give it to the house that's feeding you.

You have to understand this and get it down in your spirit. If you're thinking, "Well Pastor I started giving sacrificially," that's great, now expect a harvest. The second half of this is not just to tell you to give. The second half, if I don't tell you to expect, you will never receive. Once you understand that you are a tither, you should walk into every car dealership if you need to buy a car and say, "I know I'm going to walk out of here with a deal that nobody else will get." They can tell you, "Well you know, we don't normally do that..." but today, they're going to do something different. Why? You just stepped in the building.

You can think that's arrogance, but I think it's confidence. I think it's believing that my God shall supply *all* of my need. If I have to do what everybody else has to do, then why do I need God? If the Bible says I'm a delightsome land and people will call me that, then that means I should walk in unusual favor. That means that when you see me you should say, "Wow, God does stuff for him!" If that's the case, and God is no respecter of persons, then everything that I'm telling you that I'm confident about, He will do in your life, too. The only difference between me and you is that I expect it, I demand it, and I accept nothing short of it.

If I have to wait, I'll wait. However, there will come the time when I will see a God deal. When people look at what we pay in rent for our church building, people are shocked. We talked to realtors who asked, "Well what are you paying now?" We told them and they said, "Really? Well who did you rob to get that?" I'll tell you who I *didn't* rob to get that. I didn't rob God, so He's on my side. "I don't think you're going to get another deal like that," some could say, but the devil is a liar because God will take care of and supply all of our need. I won't move until I see a God deal. I expect it, don't you? You do now.

Ecclesiastes 11:4

"He that observeth the wind shall not sow; and he that regardeth the clouds shall not reap."

The word "observe" is "shamar" which means "to look narrowly, to regard, to wait and to watch." The word for "he that regardeth the clouds" means, "to perceive, to foresee or to look on." So what this is saying to you is he that observes the wind and stops because of the wind will not sow, and whoever regards the clouds will not reap. It's telling you that whoever takes account of what's happening naturally before you sow will never reap because you won't do it if you're always waiting on the "perfect" conditions.

See, if you see your finances and start thinking, "Oh my God I don't think I can do this. I don't see where this is coming from," you will not reap. Now there's wisdom that has to be applied in all of that, but what he's telling you is you have to be careful because Satan will squeeze you to keep you from giving. The offering comes around and you have a number in your head. You write that out, but you start thinking, "Wait a minute, I've got to buy _____ this week and I've got to do _____" and you start backing down. What Satan's trying to do is make you observe the wind. He's trying to convince you to observe the clouds and look at natural things. When you regard the natural things you will not reap a harvest because all you're focused on is your problems, your issues, your challenges, and you're not even realizing that the God who formed it in the first place will prosper you.

The reason why he said, "No weapon formed against you shall prosper," is that God is the one who made the ironworker who forged the weapon. That's what he's trying to tell you. No weapon formed against you will prosper because even if it's formed against you, God made the one who formed it in the first will allow to come near you when you trust Him. God might be trying to bless you by telling you to give it, but because you look at the world and say, "Well I don't think I can," you refuse to give it and your blessing is locked up in your stubbornness and disobedience. God does not want you to look at the circumstances.

He wants you to trust Him. Why does He ask you to tithe? So that you'll trust Him. However, here's what some people will do; "I paid my APS bill, my charge cards, and then if there's 10% left over I'll go ahead and give that." If you make decisions like that, just keep it. I know no preacher in America would tell you to keep your money, but keep it. You want to know why? It does not help you. If I'm going to tell you to do something I want to see it help you. When you start seeing that your bills are constantly being paid on time, you have cars or houses that are paid for, then you realize, "Wait a minute, you mean to tell me that God will really supply?" Yes, He will but He will not do it if you're constantly worried about the wind.

In Matthew 14 when Peter stepped out of the boat, he was doing just fine. All of a sudden the winds kicked up, the waves started to shake. The word used was "seismos" for "storm". That was not just your average storm with a little bit of wind and rain, it was a full-blown tsunami. When he took his eyes off of Christ and started looking at the circumstances, he sunk. Jesus saved him, and of course He asked Peter, "How come you doubted?" He was doing just fine. He had enough faith to step out of the boat, but he did not have enough faith to finish the journey.

If you observe the wind and regard the clouds, you'll never sow and you'll never reap because you're constantly looking at what's happening in the world. We are not to look at what happens in the world, we don't regard the wind and the clouds. What we look at is what God said to do. Now if you're not clear on what

God told you to do, then wait until you gain some clarity. Not on your tithe, that's made clear in the Bible. I'm talking about when you go beyond that as God leads you. Let Him lead you. I promise you when you plant seed and you disregard the "clouds" and the "wind", you will find those moments are when God was trying the most to send a blessing to you.

Every time God wants to move, Satan tries to move with Him. The goal is to create a facsimile that creates enough noise to distract you from what God is doing at the time. Have you ever been driving down the highway, your exit is coming up, and then your favorite song comes on the radio? You turn up the volume and boom, you miss your exit. Now you have to go the long way around. That's what Satan's trying to do to you every chance he gets. He wants you to observe the clouds and the wind, because if he can convince you to look at that then you can find all other reasons not to attend church or give.

Listen, I have just as many reasons as you do not to show up to service. Some of the TV shows you want to watch, I want to watch. Some of the places you want to go, I want to go. The reality is I understand that my supply is demonstrated by my fidelity and commitment towards God. I'm planting seeds when I show up, when I give and when I'm diligent and stand in the face of the wind and I'm still going to do it even if I had to walk to church. This is where the rubber hits the road because what you see on the flip side is everybody's complaining; "How come I don't have the blessings in my life? How come I don't have this in my life?" You don't have it because you refuse to give it. You need something to help induce labor because you're holding onto it as if you don't want to let go. The problem with that is, it does not belong to you.

Haggai 1:2

"Thus speaketh the Lord of hosts, saying, 'This people say, The time is not come, the time that the Lord's house should be built.' Then came the word of the Lord by Haggai the prophet, saying, 'Is it time for you, O ye, to dwell in your cieled houses, and this house lie waste? Now therefore thus saith the Lord of hosts; Consider your ways.'"

The people were saying the time had not yet come to build the temple (the house) for God. God responded and said, "Yet you feel the time has come for you to live in a fancy house?" In other words, He's telling them to think about and consider how they're handling things. Be circumspect for a moment and think about how you're handling things. It shows you He fully expected them to take care of His house first.

He didn't say "I'm going to leave you to die." If they took care of His house, then He is now obligated to take care of their houses. Here's the problem that people don't see. They only take care of their house therefore they only get their result. Now if you really want something, I don't want my result in my house because I only have a finite amount of resources. The result I want is God's result because He has all the resources. The Bible says all the silver and all the gold belongs to Him. The cattle of a thousand hills belongs to Him. He's the one who has it all, so if I would put what I have into Him, then He will put what He has into me.

Verse 6 says, "Ye have sown much, and bring in little; ye eat, but ye have not enough; ye drink, but ye are not filled with drink; ye clothe you, but there is none warm; and he that earneth wages earneth wages to put it into a bag with holes." When He said, "consider your ways," then he goes on to tell you if you're living hand to mouth, if you have clothes but they're not keeping you warm, if you feel like you're making money but it's constantly

ing through your pockets as if you have holes in them, if you feel like you don't have enough to eat, if you feel that you are sowing and working and giving and trying hard, but you are getting little, He said to consider your ways. In other words, think about something.

What are you to think about? How are you treating God's house? Could it get any clearer? If you're struggling with lack, consider your ways. If you don't have enough to eat, to live, to supply, to keep you warm — if you feel like every dollar you make just flies out as fast as it came in, consider your ways. Verse 7 says, "Thus saith the Lord of hosts; Consider your ways." He says it a second time! "Go up to the mountain, and bring wood, and build the house; and I will take pleasure in it, and I will be glorified, saith the Lord. Ye looked for much, and, lo it came to little; and when ye brought it home, I did blow upon it. Why? saith the Lord of hosts. Because of mine house that is waste, and ye run every man unto his own house." He said because you wouldn't put His house first, the very little you had, He blew it out of your hands. God, Himself is working against the person who refuses to take care of Him.

He did not say, "I let Satan rob you." He said, "Because you wouldn't take care of me and it's mine anyway I blew on it." You come home from the bank counting your paycheck, walk in the door and God blows it right out of your hand. He said when you brought it home, He blew on it. Everybody's going to ask, "Why would God do such a thing?" His house is in waste. You run every man to your house, but you've forgotten. He said therefore the heaven over you is stayed from dew.

You know what "stayed" is? Let's say you have little Fido, a puppy, and you tell him to stay. What does he do? When he stays, if he follows the instruction, he doesn't move. He said the heaven over you is stayed and it will not drop dew. You cannot disregard the things of God and expect to pray your way through it, or out of it. If God said this is what happens, despite your prayers, despite your complaining, despite your moaning, despite your "God knows my heart" speech — the heaven over you is stayed from dew until you recognize your responsibility concerning God.

He said, "The earth is stayed from her fruit and I called for a draught upon the land, upon the mountains, upon the corn, upon the new wine, upon the oil, upon the ground which bringeth forth, upon man, upon the cattle, upon the labor of your hands, upon everything that touches your life. I have called a draught upon it until you regard me." If you don't put God first, how am I to pray for your finances when the heaven over you is stayed from dew because you don't trust God? You're saved, going to Heaven, but living in Hell all the days of your life. He said, "I will stop the cattle, the work of your hands, everything," because you don't regard His house. What do we do with that? It's scripture, isn't it?

Luke 15:11-13
"And he said, A certain man had two sons: And the younger of them said to his father, Father, give me the portion of goods that falleth to me. And he divided unto them his living... And not many days after the younger son gathered all together, and took his journey into a far country, and there wasted his substance with riotous living."

Did the older son ask for it? No, the younger son did, but the father divided everything to both of them. Did the younger son gain any more by asking for his inheritance? No, he already had it, he was a son living with his dad. He had all the blessing. His father had to split it in half; half to one son and half to the other. So it wasn't that he wanted money, he wanted control over it. When you understand this parable there's a lot here. It's a lot deeper than just the salvation and the son coming home. It's the understanding that everything you have was given unto you by God himself. You are no more blessed by controlling it than you are having access to it.

As long as he stayed under his father's auspices he had access to the inheritance. He didn't want access, he wanted to control how it was spent. Once it was no longer under the auspices of his father, it was no longer blessed because it did not belong to him. When people think the money belongs to them, they refuse to give it to God and they'll spend it on other things because they want complete control over it. They'll spend it on drugs, alcohol, riotous living and squander the very gift that God has given them and wonder why it is dwindling away. If you want to control it, then God can't. He'll let you, but understand, it does not belong to you.

One-hundred percent of everything you have (the breath you draw right now, the roof you sleep under, the car that may be a hooptie or a Bentley — whatever you have) God gave it to you and He allowed you to keep it for His purposes and His glory. He didn't ask for all of it, He asked for ten percent of it. When you make the decision that all of it belongs to you and you won't give Him what belongs to Him, you will never completely enjoy it because you will squander it while trying to control it. See, if I leave it under my father's auspices I still have access to it. He was no more richer by asking for the money. He did not increase in wealth in his substance by asking for the money. It didn't say it multiplied when his father handed it to him, it was the same, but because he desired to control it he lost it.

Stewardship is the recognition of your responsibility for everything God's given you, whether you think you're responsible or not. Some people complain about everything. "I don't like my living situation, I don't like my house, I don't like my car, I don't like…" but if you were a proper steward over that, you would ognize that God will never trust you with a mansion if you can't take care of the apartment.

You are a steward over your relationships, your family, and your finances. You are responsible to manage these things not for yourself, but for God. You are not in control, but you have access. If God can't trust you with the girlfriend you have now and you're asking Him for a wife, then you need to act like a husband and take care of the relationship you currently have. If you want good friendships, steward the friendships that you have now. Why would God give you a greater degree of friendship or relationship if you can't steward what you already have because you're dissatisfied?

"I don't like my car. It knocks when I drive and I have to pick it up and run with it like Fred Flintstone." Are you a good steward? Do you recognize the responsibility that is given to you through access? If you want to control it, it will not last. This is the problem; the younger son went out and spent all of it by living his way. Now eventually, the Bible says that he came to his senses when he was in the pig slop with the pigs thinking to himself, "My dad's servants live better than this."

You are children of God so you are his sons and daughters. You are not just a servant to God, you're His child. This guy said his dad's servants lived better than that and *he* was his child! How much more should I live if I understand who I am through my access? He returned home to his father and the older brother became mad and asked, "Why are we throwing all this celebration for him? He's the one that left."

What was he mad about? He received his inheritance, too. I can understand he would be ticked off if his dad said, "I'm going to hold onto yours but I'm going to give him his." However, he gave both of them everything. Perhaps he was jealous he did not live the way he wanted to live. I don't know. My point is, you must consider your ways. Think about how you deal with the things of God. It's very difficult when people want me to pray for their finances or do something for them when I know they're squandering it.

It's hard to come into the church and ask for money, but yet you spend it in the casino and drink it up. It does not make any sense. Obviously we'll do whatever we can to help, but you have a responsibility to consider your ways because we are not here to support your gambling and drinking habit, your drug problem, your philandering or bad behavior. We're not here to support your riotous living. There are those who are doing what they need to do and will reach a point where they have more month than money, and we help them because that's what we do. It's the truth, and the truth shall set you free.

STEWARDING
Time, Treasure, and Talents

Genesis 2:3-16

"And God blessed the seventh day, and sanctified it: because that in it he had rested from all his work which God created and made. These are the generations of the Heavens and of the earth when they were created, in the day that the Lord God made the earth and the Heavens, And every plant of the field before it was in the earth, and every herb of the field before it grew: for the Lord God had not caused it to rain upon the earth, and there was not a man to till the ground. But there went up a mist from the earth, and watered the whole face of the ground. And the Lord God formed man of the dust of the ground, and breathed into his nostrils the breath of life; and man became a living soul. And the Lord God planted a garden eastward in Eden; and there he put the man whom he had formed. And out of the ground made the Lord God to grow every tree that is pleasant to the sight, and good for food; the tree of life also in the midst of the garden, and the tree of knowledge of good and evil. And a river went out of Eden to water the garden; and from thence it was parted, and became into four heads.The name of the first is Pison: that is it which compasseth the whole land of Havilah, where there is gold; And the gold of that land is good: there is bdellium and the onyx stone. And the name of the second river is Gihon: the same is it that compasseth the whole land of Ethiopia. And the name of the third river is Hiddekel: that is it which goeth toward the east of Assyria. And the fourth river is Euphrates. And the Lord God took the man, and put him into the garden of Eden to dress it and to keep it. And the Lord

God commanded the man, saying, Of every tree of the garden thou mayest freely eat."

The first job God gave to man was to work, guard and protect what He gave him. It's interesting to see how people live today. If you find a man that has a hard time working, you need to run. If (in his mind) work means playing video games and sitting around while accomplishing nothing all day, then ladies, you ought to run. I don't mean walk, I mean *run.* The first thing God did was give man a job, and that job is to dress it and to keep it; to protect it and to work the land.

When you understand that you're a steward, you see the basic premise when God created the garden of Eden. The garden of Eden was not a desert place, it was endued with jewels and gold; it was a well-established and well-provided for place. God's desire for you is to be successful and to provide you with all the things that you want in your life.

I think some people have a twisted doctrine where they feel God's desire is for you to be poor. Still, we see throughout the Bible that God always provided in a very — what we would call "lavish way". What if you walked into a house and it was laden with onyx and gold? You would then know that whoever built the house cared about it. So when God built the garden of Eden and put man in it, He did not put man into a state of lack. He put man into a place of abundance and told him to be responsible for it.

The garden of Eden is a place of plenty, supply, abundance, more than enough— a place of excess if we can say it that way. He said that your job is to work it and to protect it. That is the beginning of all stewardship. It starts with recognizing that what God has given you is not yours. It is His and He's given you the responsibility to work it and to protect it. People think, "Well my check is mine. I worked hard for it and I earned it." If you didn't wake up and breathe that morning you wouldn't have earned anything. There's a reality that has to be always seen, it is that everything you have in your life has been supplied by God. The fact that you're drawing breath right now has been supplied by God.

There's a joke about two scientists who got together and said, "God, we don't need you anymore because we've learned how to clone and make man." God said, "Really? Let's go ahead and have a contest. You make a man, I'm going to make a man and let's see who finishes first." So the scientists go outside, they start gathering up dirt, and God says, "No, no. Get your own dirt."

No matter how technologically savvy or intelligent you think you have become, nothing you have belongs to you. Everything you have, God blessed you with and permitted. The very basis of seedtime and harvest, of walking in any level of prosperity, is to know that what you have does not belong to you.

Let's move off of the topic of money for a minute because it's not just about money. People will take their talent to work for IBM because that company can pay them $60,000 - $80,000 per year. However, the church needs their help, but the church can't pay what IBM can— not that the church does not want to, but they don't tithe to the church (it's an interesting circle) so they will not bring it to the church; they'll work for the highest bidder. They're not being a proper steward of the gift God put in them. If you have a talent, a skill or an ability, God put that gift in you.

That's why you see a lot of people, particularly in the music industry, try to make it in the Gospel music industry. They find success in the church, cross over into secular music, go worldly, smoke as much crack as they can, and then die. Why do these them, and anything you mishandle or misuse you will not keep for long. If you can't appreciate where you are today or have respect for what God has given you, you will never progress any further. It's like giving an ungrateful child a toy. You don't feel warm and fuzzy about trying to buy them the next thing they want if they're unwilling to appreciate the things you already gave them.

How did we get to a place where people, in order to be successful, feel they have to leave the church and take the gift God gave them into the world? It happens all the time. It's improper stewardship of the resources God has given. You'll spend your time elsewhere, but when the church needs your help you refuse to invest into God's work. You are to steward your time, talent and treasure, and you are responsible for it. God gave it to you and His command was to dress it and to keep it; to work it and to protect it.

The American Heritage Dictionary of the English language defines a steward as "one who manages another's property, finances or affairs; one who is in charge of the household affairs of a large estate, club, hotel or resort". A steward is someone who understands that which they have does not belong to them; they are merely a manager of it. They are responsible for its success, failure, and correct usage. They are responsible for the time, treasure and talent. It's not just about money. How do you steward your life? If you're a good steward of your life, God commands your life.

It is amazing to me how many people claim Christ as their savior, that they are led by God and claim that God is blessing their life, yet they live like Satan. How is that possible? You have a responsibility to steward your reputation, your life, and the gift that God put in you. It's amazing how many people have a gift of God in them but cannot seem to walk it out. They cannot walk it out because they don't steward the gift that's in them. They don't tect it, and they don't work it. They're too busy in strife, contention and knowing all things great and small, so they live a life of mediocrity at best. Then, they die never having fulfilled their call from God.

Years ago, I knew a man who observed how I served my pastor. He walked up to me and said, "God told me to do the same thing for my pastor, but I just can't do it. How do you do it?" I said, "The first thing I'll tell you is I died to whatever I wanted. I'm willing to do whatever it takes." He died about 2-3 years after that having never fulfilled his purpose in Christ.

The worst thing in the world is a life wasted, not realizing that you could have done something significant. You could have been a contender. You could have been all that God wanted you to be, but your stubbornness, arrogance, and inability to submit and honor prevented you from walking in the fullness that God had for you.

He said he knew God told him to do it. You should have seen the look in his face and I felt so sorry for him. It's one thing to miss your opportunity because you don't know what God wants you to do, but it's another when you miss it and you *know* what God told you to do. That's the worst to me. I'd rather miss it and not know I missed it. You'll find out when you get to Heaven, but at least you'll be there. I'm not talking about whether you have salvation or not. We understand when you're saved, you're saved. What I'm talking about is walking in the fullness of God's perfect plan.

We're supposed to be responsible stewards of all that God has given us. If He's placed the gift in us, how dare we come to the point where we use the gift for the world and not realize that it is our job to work it and to protect it. How do we protect it? We keep it under the auspices of God and we bring it to God's table. You'd be shocked how many people refuse to do it. That's why the Bible says many are called, few are chosen. It's very disrespectful to God for you to not steward your gift, not realizing that He gave it to you.

The Bible says that before you were born He knit you in your mother's womb. He designed you and created you. You are fearfully and wonderfully made. The craftsmanship that God put into you, the thought and understanding that God put into you — when you understand that God knows how many hairs are on the top of your head, that God collects your tears in a jar, how can we not have the understanding that there's an expectation upon our lives? We ought to feel compelled to say, "I have to do what God asked me to do. I don't have much of a choice."

Realistically, it's impossible for me to sit idly and allow my life to pass by without having it consecrated unto the purposes, plans and pursuits that God has given me. How about you? When you understand you're a steward, you realize everything in your life (your gift, your talent, your treasure and your time) was given to you to do two things; to work and to protect. Some of you have a gift and you know what God wants, what He's prompted you to do, and you know what God has deposited in your heart. He's given you a passion and a fervor for it, but you've let other people steal it because you did not protect it.

You live constantly with a daydream of "one day I will preach to gazillions…" yet you don't work towards it. Now you have a vision without work (which becomes a nightmare). You have a responsibility to protect it and to work it. You did not get a free pass because you became a Christian. Some people, when they hear the word "faith" think it means they can sit back and wait for God to do it, but the devil is a liar.

The Bible says that there is such a thing as demonic faith. The demons know there is a God and tremble, yet they produce nothing good. To sit and know that God is real and to have faith that there is a God without any level of corresponding action is what the Bible calls demonic faith. Real faith is when you will do whatever it takes to accomplish the mission, the purpose and the plan that God has predestinated for you since the very foundations of the world. It means you are after it like a puppy playing with a chew toy— you refuse to let it go. You are pedantic and one-minded about it. You are all about the things of God; not about how many vacations you can take. You're not complaining about being too fatigued to attend prayer nights and family nights at the church. If you are tired, you are operating under the wrong yoke because you cannot tell me that to serve God's people you are going to be tired from loving on God. How does that wear someone out?

When you have a God-sized vision a lot of decisions in your life are made for you. I don't wake up and say, "Am I coming to the church today or am I not? Do I have to get my job to give me Wednesdays off or not?" I wouldn't take a job that made me work Wednesday nights or Sundays. It's not even an option or a thought in my head because I have a God-sized vision and I understand how I regard my God.

I went to Bible college but that didn't stop me from showing up on Wednesday. Nothing I do will ever keep me from being where God placed me. I recognize I have a supply. I understand my supply and where I'm supposed to be. I don't have problems showing up where I'm supposed to be. It's funny how people want to be in ministry but don't show up, as if ministry starts in their house while they're sitting on their couch watching their TV (TBN no doubt) getting spiritual. It is important to learn that a steward must follow the instructions they have been given or else they're make a mess of things. The most fundamental challenge that we face in regards to Christian stewardship is that human beings are always turned in upon themselves with lives that revolve around what they want, what they need and what they are concerned about ever since the fall into sin. It's an inward-focused life.

When man was separated from God by sin, now who do you turn to? When your relationship is severed with the one who created you, now you have developed a mentality that you are on your own. The problem is for thousands of years, that mentality's been beat into us. Then here comes Jesus and He says, "You know what? I just reconciled you back to your father. You now have a relationship where your daddy is providing for you." You now have that reconciled relationship in which you can trust that God of Abraham, Isaac and Jacob, now that relationship becomes primary.

However, if you still act old school and think, "I'm on my own, I have to provide for myself. Pastor, you don't understand, I have to go to work," then do that. When you fall sick and ill, ask your job for healing. When your finances go awry, ask them to front you the money you need. The reality is if you are not clear about the God you serve, you will constantly use the world as your source, but the world makes a terrible source. As the saying goes, "money makes an excellent slave, but a terrible master."

For me, money is not my master. If I have it in my bank account, I'll still be at church Wednesday nights. If I don't have it in my bank account, I will still be at church on Sunday morning because I know what is and what is not eternal. I know that situations are subject to change with one word from God. All you have to do is hear one word that brings revelation that will leap in your belly like Elizabeth's baby did. All you have to do is hear something that clicks for you to bring about a revelation that will take you to the next level with God. Your finances will then be you try to fix spiritual problems by natural means you will have turned inward and most people, when all the proverbial nonsense hits the fan, will turn inward instead of upward. It's a sign of spiritual immaturity. It's hard to put people in ministry when they're immature.

Luke 15:11-13

"And he said, A certain man had two sons: And the younger of them said to his father, Father, give me the portion of goods that falleth to me. And he divided unto them his living. And not many days after the younger son gathered all together, and took his journey into a far country, and there wasted his substance with riotous living."

We understand the above verse to be the story of the prodigal son with themes of redemption and salvation, but I want to take this a different direction. First of all, the one younger son asked for the inheritance that was going to fall to him when the father died. The father then gave not only *him* his inheritance, but he gave *his other son* his inheritance as well. Up until this point the son is living with his father and he has access to all that the father has. Once he split it between the two sons, the younger son received his half. He did not prosper, receive, or grow anymore. The money was not the motivation for him asking for all that belonged to him; it was control. He was tired of dad having it and he decided he was okay with access but would rather have control. He didn't want to keep his money in a bank account, he was happy storing it in a mattress. He had a desire to have control and the Bible says he spent it all on riotous living.

When you recognize you're a steward, you don't need control because God has control, you care that you have access. The moment you desire to have control, you will lose it all. Can God bring it back around? Sure He can. The question is how many you want to go through that before you realize you're better off leaving it in your Father's account and using the debit card? If you want the control, you will miss it.

You know, people run around saying, "I don't know about that Christian stuff. I just want to be free to do whatever I want to do." It is so bizarre how people say things like that when it's the furthest thing from the truth. They are not free. The Bible says they live according to the course of this world. A course is a laid out path. Let's say I have a maze and I put a mouse in it. The mouse goes running through the maze, but that mouse can only travel within the maze. He's not free. People in the world are not free. They think they're free but they're moving in accordance with what the world wants for them.

Whom the Son sets free is free indeed. That's who's free. So how do we bring ourselves to a place where we understand that in Christ you have a responsibility to steward that which God has given you, and that there are repercussions to bad stewardship?

Malachi 3:8
"Will a man rob God? Yet ye have robbed me. But ye say, Wherein have we robbed thee? In tithes and offerings."

If you come to my house take my car, you have robbed me. If you go to my neighbor's house and take their car, you have not robbed me. In order for me to be robbed the underlying premise, or requirement, is you will have to have taken something that belongs to me and remove it from my possession for use that I did not authorize. So if I entrusted a gift to you and you use that gift for purposes that I did not authorize, you robbed me.

If I owned a prosperous store and you worked at that store, but you steal money off the top like the old Bugs Bunny cartoons, "One for you, one for me. One for you; two for me..." You've robbed me, have you not? The money came from the customer, but did you rob the customer? No, the money belongs to the store owner. So therefore when God put gifts in you, gives you finances, blesses you with a job (whether you like the job or it makes the money you want to make), when you are in a position to have something that God has allowed you and blessed you to have, He has an intended use for it.

Your tithe is ten percent of your paycheck. Take your paycheck, move the decimal point one number to the left; that's ten percent, that's what you give. It's funny how people have a hard time calculating ten percent, but if you tell them they receive twenty-five percent off their new dress, that new pair of shoes, or that new car, then they can calculate that quickly. For some reason people struggle with ten percent. Not only did He say give your tithe, but He also said give your offerings. If you don't believe that it belongs to God then how could you rob Him if it didn't belong to Him? It's not possible.

He said, "You robbed me." They're wondering, "How did we rob you? We didn't take nothing from you." They spent what they had on what they wanted. Therefore, they felt they didn't rob the church since they didn't go in there and hold them up. They think they just spent what they had on what they wanted. God wanted to let them know that what they had belongs to Him. You are just responsible to steward it.

Malachi 3:9 goes on and says, "You are cursed with a curse for you have robbed me even this whole nation." How do we overcome that? He said because you won't take care of God, His house, He said you are cursed. How do you think you can progress financially or in anything concerning God when God himself says you are cursed?

If Satan says you're cursed, you can run to God. God can say you're blessed and that remedies that situation. However, where do you go when God himself says that? What supreme power do you know and I don't that allows you to usurp what God has said?

The same measure in which you come to God with is how you get it back because the reality is you can't come to God and say you don't tithe but still want to prosper; you are cursed. I want you to prosper beyond your wildest dreams, but you cannot do this being sloppy and disrespectful concerning what God has done for you. You have an obligation to God.

The grace message has propagated the entire world. It's a message that says you do what you want and God's okay with it, but I assure you, the fall of that will be great. It's just a matter of time. If God said it and He said, "I change not" (Malachi 3:6) it's still an issue. God brought up the tithe in the first place to see your heart. It's to see what you believe more in; APS or Him? Your landlord or Him? Who do you trust more? "Well God knows my circumstances and He knows if I had it I would." You do have it and you won't. The whole premise of "If I had it I would," implies that what you do have does not belong to Him.

It is my desire that you do not struggle. You can mark my words, in the next six months or so you're going to see the economy take another hit. If you don't learn how to do this God's way it's going to be a problem for you. You can call it whatever you want to call it and say whatever you want to say, but the goal for me is not to teach you how to swim while you're drowning. My goal is to teach you how to swim before you get in the water.

Do you know why lifeguards carry buoys? They are not soft, spongy or made of rubber, they're hard. One of the things lifeguards are trained to do (particularly in the ocean) is smack you on the back of the head with the buoy (subsequently knocking you out) in the case that you are wailing and flailing. That way they can pull you to safety so you both don't die.

If you're in the water freaking out, you both could drown. Imagine this book is that buoy and I'm trying to knock you out so you don't drown and take everybody with you. If you hear what I'm telling you it'll click for you and this is the only place where God said to prove Him and test Him.

Malachi 3:9-10
"Ye are cursed with a curse: for ye have robbed me, even this whole nation. Bring ye all the tithes into the storehouse, that there may be meat in mine house, and prove me now herewith, saith the Lord of hosts, if I will not open you the windows of Heaven, and pour you out a blessing, that there shall not be room enough to receive it."

That word, "open up the windows of Heaven" is the same illustration that would be used if you had a grain shoot. The release lever is what God is talking about. He said if you refuse to honor God in tithes and offerings, if you are robbing Him, then you are operating in a curse where the window is shut. The blessings are still coming because He's a good God, but you will not receive them until you act right concerning Him. The moment you do, all that was backed up, He'll release and it will come pouring in to such a degree that you will not have enough room to contain it.

When people read this they think, "Well if I tithe then God will just heap blessing." No, when you don't tithe, your blessings are stayed until you do. This might be semantics for some but if you get this it will answer your question as to why you have more month than money, why you have more need than supply. He says in verse 11, "And I will rebuke the devourer for your sakes, and he shall not destroy the fruits of your ground; neither shall your vine cast her fruit before the time in the field, saith the Lord of hosts." The Lord gave me an understanding of this scripture that has changed me completely. He said that the fruit shall not cast on the vine before its time in the field.

I personally love a very sweet watermelon. I think it's the worst thing in the world to taste a bad watermelon. That is a sign it didn't stay on the vine long enough. Any type of fruit that is undeveloped has not stayed on the vine long enough. The reality is if my entire crop has not matured it's not worth anything. Some of you don't understand that and you're saying, "Well I do tithe and I do give offerings yet I'm still struggling." Your fruit is still on the vine. Notice He says He will not let it cast before its time in the field. If you have grown up in the mid-west or the north-east or anywhere far north, you will know that in certain months (particularly January and February) if it becomes too warm then fruit, flowers, and plants will start to bloom. If another frost comes through in February or March, it will kill the crop because it casted its fruit before it was time.

Some people want God to move before it's their time. If God brings it before you gain revelation on how to handle it, you will go out like the prodigal son and spend it on riotous living, not realizing that He needs your revelation to exceed your manifestation so that when it comes you don't act like an Egyptian. Some people, if God dropped a million dollars in their lap right now, would have no idea what to do with it. Let me put it this way; you have no idea what's the *right* thing to do with it. Some would be driving Bentleys and still living in an apartment. "Check out my new car, Pastor!" Living ghetto fabulous.

God will not allow your fruit to cast before its time in the field. What He wants for you is ripe, sweet fruit that abounds unto your account, that you are able to not only have but to share with others. That's a time issue. How long? However long it takes for you to learn this concept. Some people think, "Well God takes forever." No, He does not.

"How come God waits until the very last minute to move? It always seems like the last moment is when God does stuff." That's the time when you finally stand in faith after you tried everything else. You made your own plans, came up with your own scheme, and nothing worked. Now you find yourself between a rock and hard place. Now you finally cry out to God with a cry of faith and He steps in and answers. That is not because He was waiting for you to be in despair, He was just waiting for you to understand Him.

God said He will rebuke the devourer and keep him out of your finances, your possessions and your home. He said, "I will rebuke the devourer for your sake." Nw we're in a whole different ball game. Maybe you don't have enough faith to rebuke Satan, but I do. Maybe somebody does not have the understanding of their authority to rebuke Satan. He said that's not even an issue because He'll do it. All you have to do is trust Him. All you have to do is say, "God here is my tithe. Here is my offering and if I do this by faith, recognizing you as my supply, realizing that I manage your estate, I manage your finances, you have given me a portion of your estate that I'm responsible for."

You are not the owner of your children; that's why you dedicate them to God. In the process of dedicating your child to God, you are giving the child to God and God's lending them back to you to raise. You have a responsibility unto God to raise them in the nurture and admonition of the Lord. That's a responsibility, that's stewardship.

You are being entrusted with their lives. You're being entrusted with a gift, a talent, a skill and finances. Everything you have, God allowed you to have. How do you get a brand new car—you're excited, been praising God and asking God for it and then somebody asks you for a ride to church and you're response is, "Not in my car!"

How do we get there, and how do we ever believe that God would bless that? We see that as so outrageous don't we, yet people still go to church, they listen to messages, they're grateful for being taught but they refuse to act on it. The more I teach on acting on the Word, the more people mysteriously stop showing up. Somehow they think if they don't hear me say it that it's not true. You are responsible for what you know. You cannot qualify for more light, revelation and understanding until you're willing to walk in the light, revelation and understanding that you already have. You won't qualify for more, that's why the Bible says you walk in the light as He is in the light.

When you walk in the light you receive more light. It's that simple. However, if you can't do what you already know to do, you will always struggle. I want you all to have blessing upon blessing, to be able to abound unto every good work. I want you to have the ability to go and do what you want without bounds to your life.

Do you want to do more, have a little bit more, and have a greater degree of freedom? If you want that, you have to understand what it takes to get there. Otherwise, I can tell you we're all great and I can teach you some principle that is biblical yet not applicable. The whole Bible is equally inspired, but not all parts of the Bible are equally important. It's a fact. If it wasn't, disciples asked, *"Which commandment is the greatest?"* Jesus would have said all ten of them, but He didn't. He said to love your God with all your heart, mind, and soul and the second is like unto the first, which is love your neighbor like you love yourself (Matthew 22:36-40).

If they all were equally important He would have said all of them, but He didn't. He said, "This is the one that is important." He knew if you did that one, you won't break the others. If you love Him, you wouldn't rob, steal, struggle against, or act out towards Him. That's what God was saying. Basically if you love Him, you'd give it to Him. You wouldn't have to struggle.

"Well I just don't see what Pastor's going to do with this money and he dresses too this and he has that…" You aren't giving it to the pastor. People allow that thought to trip them up. If you make the choice to stay poor then make it, but you won't decide that after reading this without knowing better. When God asks you why you didn't do it, you will not be able to tell Him you did not know.

You will have to read something by somebody who's afraid to talk about money. I'm not afraid to talk about money because I understand the importance of it. You can't take care of your family on little money. You need money, you have to be abundantly supplied— not because you're greedy, but because you have needs. The Lord is your shepherd, you shall not want. So many people are living below their revelation of where God wants them to be because they're unskillful in how they treat God. They're not proper stewards.

Haggai 1:7-11 NLT
"This is what the Lord of Heaven's Armies says: Look at what's happening to you! Now go up into the hills, bring

down timber, and rebuild my house. Then I will take pleasure in it and be honored, says the Lord. You hoped for rich harvests, but they were poor. And when you brought your harvest home, I blew it away. Why? Because my house lies in ruins, says the Lord of Heaven's Armies, while all of you are busy building your own fine houses. It's because of you that the Heavens withhold the dew and the earth produces no crops. I have called for a drought on your fields and hills—a drought to wither the grain and grapes and olive trees and all your other crops, a drought to starve you and your livestock and to ruin everything you have worked so hard to get."

That speaks for itself! It's heart issue, not a money issue. If it's five dollars, two dollars, or a nickel; it does not matter to God. It's heart issue. The reason He's saying "I put a drought on your life," is because you refuse to honor God. He said all you have to do is build His house. If you would build it, He will remove all the garbage off of you. You will prosper, you will bring in much, you will do fine. However, if you refuse to take care of His house while you go and build yours, He said He's going to starve you out and see who wins that battle.

I gained this understanding a long time ago and it's done me well ever since. I've come to the realization that everything God has given me, I'm responsible for. I have to be a steward of the call He's placed on my life, I have to be a steward of the gifts, finances, possessions, family and friendships that He's given me. Every single thing that God has allowed me to have, I have to steward.

I cannot allow the world to creep in and cause me to think that I have to focus more on worldly things than I do on God. It's deceptive, it's debauchery, and it's a falsehood. It's vanity to think that God is okay with us disregarding Him because He's not. He has a purpose and a plan and He needs your obedience. I can tell you one thing; if you want to find somebody who's really following the plan of God for their life, check their pocketbook.

If there's a curse in their purse, they're not following God. If you're willing to support what God is doing there's no end to where He can take you. I made a commitment and I told God I will be a conduit of everything He gives me. Whatever it is that He gives me, if it's an anointing, I'll be a conduit of it. I don't want to hold it, keep it, or block it; I want to be a conduit for it. I want it to run through this pipe and come out the other end.

I want to be a conduit of everything God has blessed me with financially. I want to be a distribution center. I want to be a vessel where everything that comes through my life, I am able to distribute to the people who need it, want it, respect it and regard it. If I'm a conduit, it has to come through me. If it does not come through me, it is stagnant. Stagnant water develops mosquitos, algae, and disease because it's damned up. If you want to flow in the things that God has for you then you have to learn that you are not the recipient, you are the steward responsible to work to protect it.

Some people have to learn how to protect what's in their life. If you'd protect your finances and the gift that's in you, you would do better. You have to learn to work it and to protect it. It's God who gave it to you and He allows you to manage it.

Imagine that the car you own, God said, "Here, this is my car. You can drive it." The place you live in, God said, "This is my home, but I'm going to let you live in it." Would you do anything different with it? Would you keep calling your car a piece of junk if you knew it was God's and He let you have it? Every time you drive on the road and there's a problem, would you talk bad about that vehicle if you knew it was God's and He just let you drive it?

If the place where you live, if you knew that it was God's and He let you have it, would you then talk bad about it?

Sometimes we can be so dismissive in our attitude, not realizing God is intimately concerned about these details. Everything you have in your life, He gave you. The fact He allowed you to wake up today means you should think, "Today is the day I'm going to do something important. I'm going to honor God with my life and do something that makes God proud." At the end of the day, He should be able to look at you and say, "Well done." Some days you'll miss it and some days you'll get it, but you wake up the next day and you start all over again. There will come a day where you won't wake up, but you'll be standing before Him.

If you hear what I'm telling you all you'll hear is, "Well done thou good and faithful servant. You were faithful over little and now I'll make you ruler over much." If you can't wisely handle the job that pays ten dollars per hour, don't think somebody will hire you for twenty dollars per hour because they won't. If you can't handle the twenty-an-hour job wisely, if you're on your cell phone texting and the company doesn't receive their full day's work out of you, do not even look for the $40-$50/hr job. How are you going to live there if you can't handle what little God gave you?

If you can't sort the mail in the mailroom, do you think you're going to be the CEO of the company? Some people need a wakeup call. How you handle what you have now will determine how God will bless you in the future. If you're mad that you're driving that old car, you'd better become appreciative of it, otherwise you'll still be driving that old car ten years from now. You want God to give you something more? You'd better appreciate what you have. What if all you had today was what you thanked God for yesterday? Imagine everything in your life disappeared that you

HONORING
Honoring God With Your Substance

If you're not going to put God first, take care of God's house, or be responsible for what you're supposed to do in terms of your stewardship then God says He's going to cause the fields not to produce. He's going to cause the rain to be stayed over your head and He's going to put you in a place where you will not prosper. I don't know how to change that because if God is the one who put you there, there's not much we can do to help other than be obedient to what God has asked us to do.

Sometimes you see immature Christians (baby Christians) and you're not necessarily able to give them all the meat; you're not able to tell them their behavior is what's really causing the problem. They are not strong enough to hear that. We do want to help, we want to teach, and we want to develop, but being a disciple means being a disciplined one. I think we've lost the art of discipleship in the church because we seem to be afraid to teach God's principles.

Barna Group did a study from 1970 until today. They are saying that people have stopped giving to the church and they gave two reasons why. It's bizarre and it kind of shocked me, but of the two reasons they gave, the first is that people started making more money. Now, by and large, one would think that if you made more money, you'd be in a better position to give more money. However, since materialism has taken over in the church, once they had an abundance of money, in their minds there was no need for God. Therefore, there was no need to reverence God.

Now we come full-circle in a day and age where most people are getting foreclosed on and they're losing all the things that they would not consecrate to God. We have to wonder, how do we get to this place? When prosperity was easy and everybody was able to accomplish it devoid of God's efforts and intervention, then everybody was excited and they forgot all about God. Now that the world's system has turned around and came home to roost in the lives of those that trusted more in the world's system than they did in God's system, now those individuals are struggling because they have pulled God out of the mix.

The second reason why giving in the church has come to a low point is because over 50% of the church's resources are coming from people who are now 65 and over. Those that are in the age groups of 25-40 do not see the necessity, and many have never been taught the value or the responsibility of supporting a local church. So with the era of the baby boomers coming to an end and dying off, the church is now left with a new generation that has never been taught the values of what a disciplined person, a disciple of Christ, should be.

They are not taught to rely upon God and His provision in their lives and now they are devoid of the truth. So in preponderance of them and their attendance in church, they are merely attending by superstition and not by relationship. They believe that if they don't show up something bad will happen in their life and they approach God as if He's a lucky rabbit's foot.

There are people today who have never been taught discipleship and the basics of being a disciplined person. If you're reading this book, then I know you have already made the decision that it is your desire to be disciplined, to have more of God, to see more fruit in your life and be able to produce God results.

You can produce some results, but they may not be from God. Doing good is not doing God. There are people who think they can be saved by doing good. There are people who, when you ask them, "Are you going to Heaven?" They say, "I sure hope so because I try to live a good life and I try to do the best for all people that I can." The reality is they are still going to Hell if they do not know Christ because doing good is not doing God.

What I'm endeavoring to do here is to teach, instruct and help you understand that there are correct and incorrect ways to approach God, particularly concerning your finances. There are those that chase God with reckless abandon, waiting for the moment when all this finance and money will fall upon their shoulders. They will be infinitely rich and wealthy beyond all dreams and imaginations, so they can spend that on themselves and all of their lustful desire.

Unfortunately, there are preachers who promote that as though they are the instrument by which if you sow into their ministry, or give them $66.23 that somehow extreme wealth will absolutely come to you, guaranteed. That is a lie straight out of the pit of Hell. How you treat the things of God is how you will receive the things of God. If every time the offering comes up and you're one of those people that conveniently have to use the bathroom every time, you will reap that. When the building fund is underway and you feel no necessity whatsoever to become involved in moving your church into its destiny with God, you will reap the seed of that.

I don't care about the amounts and neither does God, the amount is not what's important, it's your heart. You can't put money in there, maybe put a button in there. It does not matter, just sow something. Show that you are capable of recognizing your responsibility because He says in Haggai 1:11, "And I called for a drought upon the land, and upon the mountains, and upon the corn, and upon the new wine, and upon the oil, and upon that which the ground bringeth forth, and upon men, and upon cattle, and upon all the labour of the hands." He's not talking about Satan, He said that He'll do this.

When you have not put God first, when you have not taken the responsibility for the things of God, He said "everything you have, I'm going to deal with it and you won't even be able to keep that which you do have and I'm going to keep the promise (the blessing) from reigning in your life." I assure you that this book is not meant to tickle your ears but to offend your mind to reveal your heart. It's designed to help you become aware of and understand how the God we serve deals with us, so that we may be circumspect about our lives and reflect upon Him in a way that will cause you to make adjustments.

It's very simple. I am not looking for fugitives. When I get to Heaven I want disciples. I want God to say, "You did a great job." I want to look around and see the fruit of what I've accomplished and know that I wasn't leading a church of a thousand fugitives; people who come to see the praise and worship team, run the aisles and then go home and literally fail in their Christianity. We're building winners. We're building those that want to be successful in the things of God.

We're building those that have a desire for God. They want more than what's average; to be the church, not pretend to be the church. They want to do more than just show up and look like a form of godliness but deny the power thereof. I'm talking about people that have made the decision to burn bridges and cross over into the things of God. They are not looking back because they are looking forward to the future and what God has for them. They don't want what's good, what's acceptable; they want the perfect will of God.

I assure you that those who do not will sadly be mistaken when they stand before Him and they say, "God I did this in your name." His response will be, "Depart from me you worker of inequity, I never knew you." People will be shocked when they stand before Him and He says, "You know, I wanted to bless you but you didn't let me. You didn't have to live a rough life on the earth, you could have lived a better life. You valued Maman, money, stuff, possessions and a lifestyle; you valued that more than you valued your eternity with me." These are sobering words that have accurate, biblical truth.

It's funny how today, if we in society decide we don't want to believe it, it must not be true. Truths are eternal. Biblical truth does not require your faith. What you receive from God requires faith, but God's identity (who God is, who God was and who God will always be) is not dependent upon your faith or your belief because He is God. He made Himself God.

It's bizarre how careless people are in their relationship with God, not seeing the responsibility and privilege that He has placed upon them. We're so excited to be privileged to be Christians. We can quote every promise, we understand we're overcomers, more than conquerors, and living in victory. We have all the Christian rhetoric memorized, but when we talk about our responsibilities, then we want to proclaim grace. "Well you know, God does not really mean it…"

Matthew 25:14-15

"For the kingdom of Heaven is as a man traveling into a far country, who called his own servants, and delivered unto them his goods. And unto one he gave five talents, to another

STEWARDSHIP

two, and to another one; to every man according to his several ability; and straightway took his journey."

He gave five talents to one, to another he gave two talents, and to another he gave one talent. We could make the argument that it is unfair that he had three people and gave more to one and less to the other two. However, the Bible then clarifies this happened because it was according to their several ability. In other words, it was given according to the individual. So that means this man, before he went on the journey, had enough wisdom to analyze all three people. Based on his assessment, he gave one five because he felt he would do a better job with them. He gave another man two because he felt he'd do a really good job with the two but not as good as the five. Then he gave one to the last man because he felt that he was not willing to waste all of his efforts, talents or finances into someone whom he did not feel would do the right thing with it. It was according to their several ability; not their ability to believe God, not their ability to function in what God gave them, but their ability of themselves and his assessment thereof.

Matthew 25:16-21
"Then he that had received the five talents went and traded with the same, and made them other five talents. And likewise he that had received two, he also gained other two. But he that had received one went and digged in the earth, and hid his lord's money. After a long time the lord of those servants cometh, and reckoneth with them. And so he that had received five talents came and brought other five talents, saying, Lord, thou deliveredst unto me five talents: behold, I have gained beside them five talents more. His lord said unto him, Well done, thou good and faithful servant: thou hast been faithful over a few things, I will make thee ruler over many things: enter thou into the joy of thy lord. He also that

had received two talents came and said, Lord, thou deliveredst unto me two talents: behold, I have gained two other talents beside them. His lord said unto him, Well done, good and faithful servant; thou hast been faithful over a few things, I will make thee ruler over many things: enter thou into the joy of thy lord."

In today's society, one would have to believe that if I brought you five talents, or five dollars, you would have more regard for me than if I brought you two. God is not so. God didn't ask you to be a millionaire, He asked you to be responsible with what He gave you. What we have are people who compare themselves among themselves and the Bible tells us that they are not wise. We tend to look at somebody next to us and grow jealous over what they have rather than be circumspect about what we have.

Just because God trusted this person with five talents does not diminish, in His eyes, your two talents. When you begin in your own head to think, "Maybe I'm not as qualified or as worthy because I only have two..." you disregard that your two is exactly the same amount as the five in God's eyes. When you stand before Him, He's going to ask you, "What did you do with the two?" If you only have one, "What did you do with the one?"

He will give things to you based on your several ability and if you demonstrate your ability to fund the kingdom and be successful in the things of God then He will trust you with more. You will be the one who gets the five as opposed to the two. The world thinks, "Well I only got two, maybe God does not love me as much as He loves them." That has nothing to do with it, because His response was identical.

You have responsibilities to God. Everything that has been laid out in the vision for your church, you're responsible for it. You are a part of that. Some of you have asked questions like, "How are we going to counsel people when they're going through crisis?" You. You don't think your pastor is going to counsel every single human being that comes through the doors of the church, do you? We don't have that kind of time, it's not possible. When Bible schools pop up all over the place, who do you think will teach the classes? Do you think I'm going to clone myself? No, some of those teachers are reading this right now. The vision is yet before us and it is determined by people understanding how they fit in the grand scheme of things.

When you get up in the morning and you think that your job is everything in your world, you are mistaken if you do not think first and foremost, "God, what do you want? You've given me two talents." How are you responsible with the five talents that God gave you? Some of you are more talented and gifted than others. Some of you have things that God has given you and graced you with the ability to do, yet God does not have access to it. He's the very one who placed the burning desire in your heart.

Your talents may be time, it may be treasure (your finances), it may be an actual talent. How do you steward that? How do you act responsibly for what God has blessed you with; whether you think it's one, two or five? You are still accountable for what God has given you. He said, "Because you have been faithful over little I'll make you ruler over much." If you can't be faithful in the small things, in the little stuff, then you are not going to be faithful when all hell breaks loose.

When you are looking to add people to your life, you should be watching the small stuff. Pay attention to the little things that they do, how they do it, and why they do it. How responsible they are with you when you're dating will be an indication of how responsible they'll be with you when you're married. If they cannot sponsible they'll be with you when you're married. If they cannot be faithful with little then they cannot be faithful with much.

If you can't give ten cents out of a dollar you'll never write a $100,000 check out of a million. The Bible says, "Be not deceived God is not mocked." Notice it does not tell you, "Don't deceive God," because you can't deceive God. So what it tells you to do is to be careful not to lie to yourself. The only one you're really able to deceive is yourself.

Matthew 25:24-27

"Then he which had received the one talent came and said, Lord, I knew thee that thou art an hard man, reaping where thou hast not sown, and gathering where thou hast not strawed: And I was afraid, and went and hid thy talent in the earth: lo, there thou hast that is thine. His lord answered and said unto him, Thou wicked and slothful servant, thou knewest that I reap where I sowed not, and gather where I have not strawed: Thou oughtest therefore to have put my money to the exchangers, and then at my coming I should have received mine own with usury."

I want you to notice God's response because if we apply the world's wisdom to it we probably would say, "Well at least he didn't lose the money," and that it would be good enough. However, notice God's response to this man. He said, "You could have at least, at minimum, put my money in a bank and I could have gotten a little bit of interest." Notice when God made the investment into these three individuals, He did not make the investment in order to hide the talents. In other words, God didn't make the investment into them as a safe place to store His money. That wasn't His reasoning.

He wanted them to have the ability to do something with it and bring back fruit. God's expectation was not for them to just hold on to it. His assessment of whether or not they were good and faithful or wicked and lazy was not whether they protected His money, it was how skillfully they used it to gain more fruit for the kingdom. Some of you have certain things that you are just protecting for God but you won't use it for Him. God did not ask you to keep your gift for only you.

He did not ask you to revel in the nature of your talents and abilities in your own mind. He wants you to take the gift, the talent that He has given you, and do business with it— giving Him, at minimum, some interest. He didn't say to give back what He already gave you. When you return unto God, which all of you will do, He's going to ask you, "Okay, I gave you this when you were born. What do you have for me? What did your talent produce? What did you do with the finances I gave you for the Kingdom? Is there any fruit here in Heaven because of you? Is there anything you've done to further my work on earth?"

Any time you sow into what God is doing, whether it be your time, talent or treasure, it says it abounds to your Heavenly account. Everything you do here will show up there. When He looks at your account ledger, will He see any fruit from you? Will He say, "Wow, look at this person. Look at this ministry. Look at this group of people! Look at this stuff you've affected. You've done such a good job. You took your five and you made five more. Come on in, enter into the joy of the Lord." Or not?

I want you to think about something for a minute. Could it possibly have been that this man was afraid to step out in the things of God? Could it have been because he only received one that he thought, "Maybe I'm just a screw up. I could try to do business with it, try to start a business and make some but if I lose it all this, God's going to be very upset with me." God would rather you try than sit back in the pious nature of your own mind and think somebody else will do it. The beautiful part is eventually somebody else will and they'll be the ones reaping the reward that you'll look at constantly and say "Why do they have and I don't?" It's not because they're any better than you, it's not because they're any smarter than you. They just had courage.

The end of every test is courage. Courage is the ability to stand and do, in light of fear. Courage is not the absence of fear, courage is the surmounting of fear when it is present. As a matter of fact, you cannot have courage without fear. It is amazing to me how many people do not see the responsibility that God has placed upon their lives for that which they are to do. They don't see it, they don't care, and they don't think it's important. Yet it affects every area of your life and everything you do is being gauged. Are you a five talent person, a two talent person, or a one talent person?

Matthew 25:27-30
"Thou oughtest therefore to have put my money to the exchangers, and then at my coming I should have received mine own with usury. Take therefore the talent from him, and give it unto him which hath ten talents. For unto every one that hath shall be given, and he shall have abundance: but from him that hath not shall be taken away even that which he hath. And cast ye the unprofitable servant into outer darkness: there shall be weeping and gnashing of teeth."

This is blatantly unfair. You mean to tell me that, because of how he handled what he had, God took from the man who didn't have and gave it to the one who was given more? I wanted to draw you a parable and show you some things because sometimes when I show stuff in the Old Testament people say, "Oh that's in the Old

Testament. We've been delivered by grace," but I wanted to bring something forward because these words are written in red in the Bible. If these words are written in red, this is a story that Jesus himself was telling.

He said those that don't have, what you don't have will be taken from you because you have not used it. God didn't want you to hold it, God didn't want you to put it on a shelf, polish it, and make it a pretty idol. God gave it to you to produce something. Not just anything, but something for the Kingdom. You have a unique set of gifts, talents, abilities, and personality that God gave to you. You might get on other's nerves with the gift that God gave you, but just the same, He gave it to you and He fully expects you, as a steward, to be responsible.

I think that's so unfair to say, "Wait a minute. You mean to tell me that the one who didn't have, what he did have was taken from him? Don't we give more unto the poor and don't we give more to those who have less? Don't they have a greater grace for the ones who are the unseemly parts? How do we dare judge in that situation to say that a person who has less should now have nothing?" It's all because of how they treat what they do have. That one talent guy who does not have much should have had an attitude of gratitude and said, "I'm going to do something with this," because the Lord trusted him with it. The Lord didn't have to give it to him, but He gave it to him anyway. He entrusted him with something and instead of seeing the value of what was entrusted to him, he did nothing because he was afraid.

He did nothing because he was in fear and rocked to his very core about who his master was. He was focused on the wrong thing and tried to reap where he hadn't sown. God wanted fruit that He, Himself did not have to personally bring. He wants you to bring it because He works through you. That's why you have Christ in you, the hope of glory (most of you anyway!) and it's amazing to me how people don't see that God does not care about you trying.

We, as a society, started looking at these pee-wee games with kids and started saying, "Nobody's a winner, nobody's a loser. Everybody won!" What's the score? We don't know. I understand why they did that, but that mentality created the workforce that we have today that thinks as long as they try, they deserve a paycheck. The truth of the matter is (from an employer standpoint) nobody cares that you tried. They can't pay their bills with your trying. What they look for are your results.

Have you produced an outcome that you desire? Have you produced fruit? "But I'm trying, mommy!" That is great when it comes out of the mouth of babies, but those that have put away childish things must come to the understanding that it is not that you try that reaps the reward. We praise effort, "Good boy Johnny. That's a good job, you're trying," but we reward the results. If you don't hear that, you'll be developing the next generation to believe that they can receive a reward just because they tried. They'll be relegated to a life of jumping from job to job and their response will be, "Nobody appreciates my gift or my talent," when the reality is they don't have any or the only one that they have, they will not use it for the common good of the institution in which they work.

That's why they're not seen as valued. Any employee that is seen as valued, a company will do whatever it takes to keep them if their perceived value is high enough. It's a fact. You must understand that in the real world, God's world, He is not looking for you to try. He's looking for you to *do*. The moment you do, He supplies the outcome and you supply the doing. That's the essence of faith. That's the whole nature of why we confess by faith that we believe in our God.

The Christian community is literally overwrought with people who are constantly being endorsed, rewarded, and encouraged not to do but to try. When I come with the understanding that I'm going to try, I am not assured by faith of my outcome that I *can* do. Trying within itself has an element of fear that I will not accomplish that which I've set out to do. We don't try, we do and when we do we see fruit. When we see fruit, we know that God looks at us and says, "Well done thou good and faithful servant. Because you have been faithful with this, I will make you ruler over much."

Let's think practically for a minute. You have a car, but it's not the greatest car in your mind so you call it a piece of junk. You call it every name in the book. It stalls out on you one day and you're like, "This piece of garbage! I can't believe this junk..." Are you really being faithful with what you currently have? If you cannot appreciate the confines of your apartment or your house, however big or small it may be, why do you beg God to bless you with a mansion that you will be just as disrespectful with?

See, because what you have— whether you like it or not, whether you respect it or not, whether you see it or not— is given by the grace of God. If you live stuff-focused where your measure of your life will be related to the things that you have, you will never be happy, because you'll always want more. You'll always want bigger. You could get a ten foot boat and then you'll want a twenty foot boat! If you get a twenty foot boat, you'll want a forty-five foot. You'll never be happy because your happiness will be tied to things.

If your life becomes based on people, you'll never be happy because the moment they treat you the way you don't want to be treated, you'll be upset. The moment you don't get your pastor's way you think they should, your life falls to pieces. Then your attitude changes, and your life is personally affected by external influences that have nothing to do with you. The moment you make the decision not to be stuff-focused and people-centered but God and principle-focused you won't be calling your car a piece of junk and thinking God should have given you better.

How you treat your children is a reflection of the gift that you feel you've received from God. How you treat your house, your home, your family, your stuff, your possessions, your vehicles— whatever is under your authority, how you treat it is a reflection of how you see God. He expects more out of you than you expect from yourself. When you look at your gift, regardless of what the gift is, are you really, truly producing fruit? Or are you just at a place where you think, "When God gives me more, I'll just deal with more"?

Leviticus 27:30-32
"And all the tithe of the land, whether of the seed of the land, or of the fruit of the tree, is the Lord's: it is holy unto the Lord. And if a man will at all redeem ought of his tithes, he shall add thereto the fifth part thereof. And concerning the tithe of the herd, or of the flock, even of whatsoever passeth under the rod, the tenth shall be holy unto the Lord."

I want to share this with you. The rod represents authority. Spare the rod, spoil the child. What does that mean? To let them know that you are in authority. There are times in which you must take that rod and apply it to your child's "bootious maximus" until their cerebral cortex gets a new revelation. What does the rod do? It asserts your authority in their life. He says a tenth shall be brought of everything that passes under the rod. That means everything that comes under his authority, his rod, his realm, his home, his house, everything that was under his authority God his house, everything that was under his authority God expected a tithe off of.

I want you to please recognize that when I'm talking to you, I am not speaking only to your finances (as sometimes you will find that people who talk about this will only say it's about your money). It's not just about your money, it's about your time, your treasure, and your talent. How about your time? Do you give a tenth of your week to God? Or are you one of those people that just refuse to serve and help as if you think that is okay? Does God get that tenth?

Does He get one 24 hour period out of the seven days that you have, or do you just put in fifteen minutes and that has to be good enough? All that passes under your authority, God expects you to be responsible for. "Well I've got a job, I've got stuff to do and I'm busy and I go to school and I feed the hungry and the poor and I take care of Mother Teresa even though she's been dead. But I do all this stuff and…" You come up with a list of things that you have do because you're busy. Busy, busy, busy. All the while God is asking you what you're doing with everything that came under your rod, your staff; your authority.

What are you going to do when He comes back to reckon? What are you going to do when He asks you for an account of what has occurred? How do we respond when we know that we didn't do what we're supposed to do? Now will you make it to Heaven? Of course you will, but is our primary goal to arrive there, or to be pleasing unto the one who left us here for a while? Some of us will be here on this planet longer than others, but God left you here in the time that you have and He told you to redeem the time.

The Bible tells us to teach us to number our days so that we may apply our hearts unto wisdom. There is only but a finite ber of days for each and every one of us. There will come a moment where your name will be called and you will have to answer for what you did with all the time you had. Were you busy?

I have a definition for that; B.U.S.Y. — *Being Under Satan's Yoke*. Satan is all too elated to give you enough distraction to keep you from being effective for God's Kingdom. If it didn't matter, why would he fight your financial contribution so adamantly? Please tell me that Satan is not smarter than we are and that we have enough sense to see it and not yield ourselves to that which he wants to do. We're responsible for everything that comes under the rod of our authority. If it's within our realm, we're responsible for it.

PROSPERING
Abounding Unto Every Good Work

You can watch these people on TV who tell you to send them $6.45 and you'll get a hundred fold blessing, a million dollars, you'll drive Ferraris, Lamborghinis, and you'll never struggle again, but that is not real, not true, and not even biblically-based whatsoever. Now let's look at the flip side because there are people who think God is glorified when you're poor. Does God want you to be poor? No. We understand that people struggle, we all struggle in various areas of our lives, but I want you to understand that God wants you to prosper.

Why does He want you to prosper? He wants you to abound unto every good work. Why does He need you to abound unto every good work? If you don't do it then who else will? God has a purpose and a plan on this planet and He needs you to help. You understand that if your finances are scattered then you are unable to help financially for the kingdom. If your health is scattered then you will not be able to help with the kingdom. Satan comes in to steal, kill and to destroy. That is his game plan, his goal, and the outcome he's looking for, but God said, "I have come that I might give you life more abundantly to the full 'til it overflows."

So if Jesus came to give us life to the full then you must understand that it is God's desire for you to prosper and not just financially but holistically. We're talking about your health, relationships, finances and emotions. God expects and desires for you to be successful, but there are rules to the game but people those rules. They see themselves in places wondering "How do we get out of there?" No matter how far you sink, God will reach down there and pull you up. Isn't that something? He does not hold grudges, He does not care. He wants you to be prosperous so if you missed it yesterday then all you need to do is make Godly choices today.

If you understand you're managing the affairs of someone else, how dare you spend money devoid of God when it's His in the first place? This is the reason why a majority of the people that struggle in their finances are doing so; because they are managing someone else's money and don't know it. If we were in businesses, the way most people live their lives, their businesses would be shut down. Most people live off of more than they are supposed to and with the advent of credit cards we have become a credit society in which the body of Christ, by and large, is in debt.

Have you ever heard of indentured servitude? It is where an individual is enslaved to someone for monetary gain. The individual would go to a master of some sort in need of money, or perhaps owed them money for something, then would have to work off the debt over a period of time. Now, the game of indentured servitude was to charge an interest level that would be so high it would never allow the enslaved person to ever pay off what they owed. Indentured servitude was done away with because someone realized how wrong that really is, then they must have come up with the credit system.

The credit system is designed to charge you an interest that you'll never be able to pay off. Now when you go to work and make a paycheck, your money goes to the Credit Company because they're the bank and you owe them. It is a modern day version of indentured servitude in this babylonian system that we live in. God is not subject to this world's system. So therefore it is in. God is not subject to this world's system. So therefore it is the blessing of the Lord that maketh rich and adds no sorrow to it.

In other words, that hard toil where you hear people saying, "I just have to get another job and another job and another job..." and next thing you know their family life suffers and their children are suffering, being brought up by television because mommy and daddy are working so hard to make a living all to keep up with the Jones' because they have compared themselves among themselves. Now a one talent is trying to keep up with the five talent and in that process they have indentured themselves to a place where they are no longer a wise steward of what God gave them.

Once you become oblivious to the fact that everything you have is to be managed like it's God's (because it is), you are destined for failure. It's what's called the bottom line for a business. The bottom line is very simple: Revenue minus expenses equals profit, period. So the question becomes, if we were to run our businesses like we run our lives, do we really live within our means? If your revenue, your income, your salary, or your paycheck is greater than your expenses (how you live and your lifestyle) then you will have a net profit. However, if your lifestyle exceeds, if you have more month than money, then you must ask yourself if your revenue exceed your expenses.

You are still responsible for that paycheck whether it's $1,000 a week or $10,000 a week. You are still responsible for what God has blessed you with; how you handle it, how you manage it, your supervisory skills, your management skills, your leadership skills... God blessed you with children, you are responsible for them whether you like it or not. You are responsible for everything that comes under your rod of authority and a proper steward understands that they must manage it not to the specifications of them, but to the one who hired them.

There was an insurance white paper that was done by Mutual America. In this white paper, they defined one of the specific things you should look for before you make anyone responsible for your will and testament. This is what they wrote, "The person appointed by a testator to execute his will or to see it's provisions carried into effect must be involved, meticulous, responsible and trustworthy."

Galatians 3:26-29

"For ye are all the children of God by faith in Christ Jesus. For as many of you as have been baptized into Christ have put on Christ. There is neither Jew nor Greek, there is neither bond nor free, there is neither male nor female: for ye are all one in Christ Jesus. And if ye be Christ's, then are ye Abraham's seed, and heirs according to the promise."

An heir is someone who is the recipient of a will or a testament. If a person dies without a will they die with what they call intestate which means they did not have a will that directs their possessions. The state steps in and now they figure out what to do and of course, nine times out of ten, the family ends up with very little after the state is done with it.

You are a joint heir because you are Abraham's seed. What makes you Abraham's seed? You believe in Christ. Once you've accepted Christ, you have now become what is called a joint heir. As a joint heir you are now responsible for the will and testament, the new testament and the old testament that God has left for you, because the word "testament" basically is a will. It's an outlining of my desires, my plans and what I would like to have happen when I go.

So I want you to understand that the Bible is the testament of God, it's the will of God exposed or revealed. So the Bible is the item that transfers understanding of what God wants from you as a joint heir. Why are you an heir? You believe in Christ. So now you have been brought into the family and given an inheritance that now empowers you to prosper. However the challenge that we have is it says because its appointment is very involved the person chosen should be meticulous, responsible and trustworthy.

1 Corinthians 4:1 AMP
"So then, let us [apostles] be looked upon as ministering servants of Christ and stewards (trustees) of the mysteries (the secret purposes) of God. Moreover, it is [essentially] required of stewards that a man should be found faithful [proving himself worthy of trust]."

If you are going to be a steward you must be faithful. Faithful is not the same as full of faith. Full of faith is one thing, faithful is another. Now let me help you understand something. You can't be faithful without being full of faith but you can be full of faith and not be faithful. If you are an heir and you are responsible for the execution of the last will and testament of God himself, then He has a responsibility placed upon your shoulders to do what He has outlined here to do with it.

Do you realize that in real life if you are the heir and the responsible testate of a person's will and you do not do in accordance with what they've asked for you can be sued because it's a breach of contract? There's a fiduciary responsibility between you and the person who's already passed. There are people who desire to be used more of God in their finances but they don't exhibit faithful characteristics. They're not committed to the plan of God for those finances. In other words you want God to bless you but the moment He blesses you, you use it for you and not what He's asked for.

Then we wonder, "Why don't we have more?" If you want more then you have to prove yourself faithful and your faithfulness is not proven in abundance, but in lack. Your faithfulness is proven when you think, "I don't have enough." Problems do not build character in your life, problems will *reveal* character in your life. You either have it or you don't. As an heir, if you are a joint heir you are responsible to execute in accordance with His last will and testament. You are responsible for what He's given to you. Every single thing that I have, God gave to me.

There is nothing that I have that is mine except my mistakes. If there's a mistake to be made then it's mine. If I did it right, it's His success. If I have it, if it's a possession, if it's on me, if it's with me, if it's around me, if I own it, if it's mine, it's because *He* allowed me. He saw enough in me to count me faithful and say, "I'm going to give you this to have."

It is not my place to look at somebody else and say, "Well how come they have this and I don't have that?" The moment you start looking at other people is the moment you take your eyes off of God. Peter sank because he took his eyes off of Christ, but when he first started out he had his eyes on Christ.

Satan will speak in your ear and start telling you, "You know so-and-so, boy they're prospering and you're not." He'll even tell you about people who don't go to church, "Look how they're prospering. They don't give, they don't do anything and they're prospering." The Bible tells you to never look at the wealth of the wicked and see them prospering and think about it. What is it to gain the whole world and to lose your soul? There will come that moment where every one of us will have to stand before God and the people who refuse and reject God; there is nothing like a fool that rejects God. When that moment comes it'll become clear to you why you had to struggle but yet God received the glory. If you derstand this you'll compare and count yourself amongst the secular world and you'll think like the secular people think.

Satan is all too willing to allow you to use your gift for his purpose. You understand, he does not have the ability to create a gift. So what he has to do is rob you of yours. If you're going to be successful long term in the things of God, the primary understanding that you must have is that you are a steward of everything you have. Everything you are, everything you're about to be, everything you own, you are a steward of it. It was left as an inheritance to you. As a joint heir you enjoy certain benefits that not everybody else has.

Now the question becomes why does the church struggle more than the world does? If you want to find the most financially strapped people, come to the church. If it's God's desire to bless us then why do we see worse degrees of wealth in the church than we do outside of the church? There's more world in the church than there is church in the world. Instead of walking by faith, we walk by sight.

If we have a million people in our church we're happy. If we have 10 people in our church we're sad about it. We're moved by what we see. If you know that you're called then you know you don't belong to yourself; you are a possession. I know some of you are thinking, "I ain't nobody's possession." You are a possession. You have been bought with a price. The blood of Jesus was shed for you, He paid the ultimate price.

It's like the joke with the farmer, the pig, the cow, and the chicken: The animals got together and said, "Lets make the farmer breakfast." The chicken's said, "That's great! Lets do it!" The cow said, "That's an excellent idea!" But the pig is sweating bullets. They ask him, "What's wrong with you?" He said, "All you've got to do is lay some eggs and give up some milk. But for me, I've got to give up my life to put bacon on that table." To give up your life is the highest price ever that has to be paid and Christ did it willfully.

The Bible says it was His passion. I don't know about you, but that changes the game a little bit because now you have a responsibility. It should be deep-seated in you to look at everything that you have, be circumspect and say, "Am I using this for the glory of God or am I using it for the glory of myself?" I'm not talking about tithing just your money, how about your time? There are 24 hours in a day, seven days in a week. Do you tithe off of your time for the work of God or do you just show up? Do you ever think to yourself that maybe God wants a little bit more? Maybe God could bless you a little bit more if you demonstrated obedience in the things He's asked you to do.

If I were your supervisor and had to run the tale of the tape of your life, would I promote you? It's a rhetorical question, something for you to think about. Would you be promoted if you had a boss over you that was looking at how you managed your life? Would they promote you? Would they give you additional responsibility?

I taught in the series "Financial Peace" about reducing 30% of your income and living off of 70%. The first 10% you give to God, the second 10% you put it into investment or a savings account and the third 10% you put in your bank account and pay yourself. Do you ever think to yourself that if you're not doing that, you are not getting paid? APS is getting paid, the mortgage company's getting paid, the landlord's getting paid, but you are not getting paid. You're making money, but you're not getting paid. You're making money and God's not getting paid if you don't tithe.

So now you have no money to invest or any type of savings. You have no money that you're paying to yourself, and you are not paying God. To me, that's an all around failure, but yet you want more. If you can't figure out how to manage what you have, why would I give you more? If you are killing my company, why would I let you run another one of my companies?

You are a steward and as a steward, you must be faithful. As a steward, you must recognize that you have a responsibility to God first, and if you want more then you must be found faithful because God will only deal with you in accordance to your ability. If He knows every time He blesses you financially you'll go out and buy two tons of Bubblicious Bubble Gum, why would He bless you again? There's a responsibility that is placed upon your shoulders as a Christian. You have a responsibility to do what is right concerning your stewardship and when you put it in its proper perspective, you will no longer think about what you want. You'll be asking God, "What do you want with this? How do you want me to do this? How do you want me to handle this situation?" Every time you do that you will see significant change.

1 Peter 4:10 AMP
"As each of you has received a gift (a particular spiritual talent, a gracious divine endowment), employ it for one another as [befits] good trustees of God's many-sided grace [faithful stewards of the [f]extremely diverse powers and gifts granted to Christians by unmerited favor]."

God tells you to use your spiritual talent, your gift, the things that He's endowed you with for the benefit of others. Your ability to affect this world (in whatever way God has designed) is captured on the inside of you. The Bible says that you were fearfully and wonderfully made and that He has predetermined and predestined you, that He had a plan and a purpose for your life foundation of the world. God thought about you from the beginning and has a plan for each and every one of us.

Do you realize there are seven billion people on this planet right now? Can you imagine how many people have lived on this planet over thousands and thousands of years? God has a specific plan in Him for each and every one of them. Could you imagine what would happen if people realized and became adequate stewards of what belongs to God? Can you think how fast the Gospel would spread? Remember, Coca-Cola did it in 20 years, now they're on every continent and in every country in the world. They were able to accomplish what the Gospel has not been able to do in thousands of years. Sugar water has done that.

Surely that cannot be because God is not all-powerful and the CEO of Coca-Cola has more abilities and skills than God. The only reason why that can happen is because Christians have not taken responsibility over what God has blessed them with and they have not used it properly. It's okay for the CEO of Coca-Cola to fly around in jets but let T.D. Jakes fly around in one and all the critics will come out. Never mind the fact that he can now travel home quickly and spend more time with his family. Why wouldn't God want to bless that man with the best technology available?

If we were to be honest, the best transportation available when Jesus walked the earth was an animal like a camel or a donkey. Jesus had them, had one that no man ever rode on before. Some people believe in theology that says Jesus was poor so everybody's supposed to be broke like it's their Christian duty. He said, "This one right here, you put this away and no man will ride on it." That would have seemed excessive in that time. People have bad theology. When the disciples were looking for tax money, Jesus told them to find it the mouth of a fish. I'm responsible with what I have and if I'm responsible in what I have, then everything I need is supplied. I understand it is my responsibility to be a steward.

You don't have to adopt any of this but I'm going to share three things with you that are personal things for me. These are just personal points for myself and the way I believe, and the way that I see it. I say that because I don't want you to think that I derived these out of scripture, although they are based on my scriptural understanding, but this is not something that comes straight out of the Bible. This is something that comes straight out of my heart.

There are three levels of stewardship in my opinion: one is ordinary stewardship, which is returning to God what He deserves out of spiritual obligation through tithes and offerings. To me that is the lowest level of stewardship; that's poverty thinking. You're not comparing yourself to me, you compare yourself to yourself not among everybody else. To me, to gives tithes and offerings is ordinary. That is not the ceiling, that is my floor.

Then there's extraordinary stewardship. This goes beyond tithes and offerings, this is where you take personal responsibility for the finances of the church and God's Kingdom and seek to funnel as much time, talent and treasure into it as possible. The last one, which is where I want to be, is called legacy stewardship.

Legacy stewardship is the opportunity to leave planned gifts that constitute both a legacy to generations yet unborn and a final witness to those whom we hold dear which continues long after we've gone home to be with the Lord. Now wherever you fit in all of that, I didn't share that with you to be condemning, to hurt your feelings or make you feel bad. I want you to see where you can go because you may find you're an extraordinary steward. Well, legacy steward is the next step.

If you're already building a legacy where you are working diligently so whatever you are doing will speak to generation after generation then you've arrived. However, if stewardship is just ordinary for you, if you're fighting to do tithes and offerings, you are living below the revelation that God has for you and you are walking in a lack that God cannot do anything with until you step up.

If you're thinking, "I'm doing fine right now," then I ask you to imagine what you could do when God can step in and give you the grace to move to the next level. It is my desire with everything that I have to bring all that I am, all that I will ever be to the plan and to the purpose of God. I want it to be something that will speak volumes of what God has done in my life, that the ripple will be so big that it'll still go on long after I'm gone.

When I look at different ministries, sometimes I wonder what happened to them. What happened to the anointing on Smith Wigglesworth? What happened to the anointing on these men and women of God that have gone on to be with the Lord while Kenneth Hagin's ministry is in 70 countries across the globe! Don't you want to do something that goes beyond just your 9-5 job? Do you want your gravestone to read, "Here lies so-and-so; they were the employee of the month three times." Will that be the moniker and your claim in your life, the extent of your value, the whole purpose of everything that you strived for in your life so that they could say you were employee of the month?

You retired early, or is the measure of your success based on you being able to do something for God that becomes a generational effect? Is that not the purpose that our God has for us? Your life is but a mist, a vapor, here today and gone tomorrow. Nobody knows the hour that cometh, nobody knows when your name will be called. So, what are you doing? I emphatically want think about what you are doing with your life. What are you doing with the gifts that God gave you?

Some of you, you're in. You're in financially, you're in with your time, you're in with your talents. Keep doing what you do. However, there are some of you reading this that know you should be in, you feel it. It's constantly tugging at you but you shrug it off thinking, "I'll get to it when it's important." All the while, God is tugging, asking, and begging, "Hey would you just listen to Me for a second? I've got a plan. I've got something for you. I know how to do this; if you'd just listen to Me I'll show you how to do this." All the while we turn our backs to Him in pursuit of things, so we miss our opportunities.

As a steward you are held responsible and you're being graded on a test that maybe you did not know about before today. However, today, my hands are clean because you will not be able to say you didn't know, because I told you. If you know me well enough you will know I am not preaching something that I don't practice. I live it because that is the way life works. I don't have another way. Sometimes I wish I did, but I don't.

All I'm trying to help you see is that when you stand before Him, I want you to hear, "Well done thou good and faithful servant." Doing good is not doing God. Doing good is fine, it's great, but if you think that everything that's good is God, you've missed it. There is a way to live this life successfully and I hope this is getting across to you.

COVENANTING
Understanding Covenant

The word "covenant" comes from the Hebrew word "to cut". In fact, the Hebrew word is spelled and pronounced like our English word. You've heard people say, "cut a deal" before, which means to come into a mutual agreement or understanding with another. Both parties have to agree. Covenant works the same way, but it cannot be broken. I'll share a fairly gruesome story to demonstrate this point:

King Xerxes had a young man that served in his army. The man's father had cut covenant with King Xerxes and the man was getting ill. He said, "Can you please do me a favor? Send my son home to take care of me, and allow him not to serve in the army." King Xerxes took the young man, cut him in half, and put him on two sides of the road. Then he took his entire army and marched them down the middle between the two pieces of the man.

Now in a minute you're going to understand technically why he did that. It's not just a cruel thing, it's a matter of understanding covenant. That's why animals were sacrificed, because what you were exemplifying is the understanding that if you broke covenant with someone, what was done to that animal would in turn be done to you. The reason he marched his men down the middle of it was to do two things. One was to let them know that covenant was serious and the second was to remind them of their covenant and what would happen.

God's perspective of covenant is not the same as your perspective of covenant. Nowadays your word (rather, the word of most people in society, really) is not what it used to be. Even if you are a person of your word, the person on the opposite end does not always believe in it. When we look at a contract, for example, the truth of the matter is a contract is only as good as the person who signed it. I don't care how ironclad it is, I don't care how many attorneys you hired; when you deal with a court case it's not about who is or is not guilty, it's about who hired the best attorney. It's sad yet true.

For some, words may be easily broken today, but covenant cannot be broken. Once covenant is broken, the offending party becomes responsible for the offense and the punishment is death. In today's day and age, let's say you made an agreement, but then decided not to honor it because the sun came out and it also rained. It could be that silly, that simple, and that easy for somebody to break their word today. The Bible says a man is to honor his word even to his own hurt, but that's not the way it is today.

People will tell you things, they will promise things, but the moment they have a wild hair, they're done. Their word is no longer valid, their agreements are no longer honored, and then we wonder why they're struggling with death (Death of finances, life, or relationships. Death is not just meaning passing from one life to the next. Death could be the death of your money, your relationships, etc). It happens if you're not an honorable person.

Covenant cannot be broken. Covenant is not an agreement, it's not a deal. It goes beyond someone only saying, "You know if you ever need something you can give me a call. I'll help you out," but then the first time you're in need, you make the phone call and they're response is, "Well you see... you know... see like... you know, I'm just saying because... but you know what I'm saying, right?" Yeah, what you're saying is that when you told me to call you, you didn't mean it. Covenant goes a step beyond an agreement.

Covenant was only cut for four reasons and they're called *The Four P's*: provision, protection, preservation, and partnership. Provision was designed to resolve lack. For example, let's say you had a tribe that knew they had a green thumb, they knew how to farm, they were agricultural yet they couldn't hunt to save their lives. So when they ran across another tribe that could hunt but couldn't grow anything, they'd cut covenant. In the one tribe they're lacking provision of meat while the other tribe lacks vegetables, fruits, grains and things of that nature. Because one lacks what the other does not, they will cut covenant with each other to provide one for the other. It becomes a provision to resolve a lack that may be prevalent in their society or group. It is very much like the covenant of marriage; a wife brings her supply and a husband brings his supply. When they bring their supplies together domestically and spiritually they form a covenant which becomes marriage. It is amazing to me how people don't understand that both parties have a responsibility to bring a supply and furthermore you have to be careful how you deal with that supply because you are responsible to bring it. If you don't bring it, 'til death do you part does not only mean when you just happen to die. Sometimes a covenant or a marriage can die because a person refuses to bring their supply and they've killed the covenant. Provision was a necessary element of covenant and there was a necessary supply that was brought by virtue of covenant. Now if you agree to bring the supply, but you later refuse to continue providing your supply, then you have violated covenant.

The second reason covenant was cut was for protection and safety. If you knew you could hunt, you could cook, you just had everything down but you couldn't fight your way out of a wet per bag, you'd cut covenant with people who know how to fight, You say, "Look, here's what we fittin' to do. We'll take care of everything around here. Somebody coming in from the outside, you protect us. As long as you protect us, we'll supply you with food, clothing, etc..." Sounds very similar to a marriage. The husband's job is to protect and keep.

The third reason for covenant was preservation. Let's say all the men of one tribe went off to war, they were killed off and all that was left were the women. The bloodline could not be continued anymore because there are no more men. So from a preservation standpoint, the tribes would form a relationship that would bring about offspring to keep the family bloodline and the family name alive. When they came together, they would exchange the last name so that you would be still within the lineage of the family so that the family would continue on. So preservation of a family, to keep the lifeblood going and to keep it moving, would become necessary to cut a covenant.

The last one is partnership. Years ago I had a person who worked with me in a mortgage company and he kept calling himself a partner. I said, "You don't understand, if you call yourself a partner why do I always have to be looking for you?" A partner shows up. A partner is the first one there and the last one to leave. If you're going to call yourself a partner to me you'd better work like I work, otherwise I'm the boss and you're an employee. If you don't have skin in the game, you are not my partner. Covenant was established by nature of partnership to ensure this one thing; that neither party would take advantage of the relationship. When you come together in covenant you are supposed to bring a certain supply and the other party is supposed to bring a certain supply.

That's why the Bible says to wives that are holding out on your husbands, knock it off because you're robbing him of his due benevolence. In other words, he has a right to it. "Due" means it belongs to somebody. When the bill is due, the collector wants their money. "Due" means it belongs to him and "benevolence" means it makes him happy. So now in order for the relationship not to be taken advantage of, covenant was cut.

Now, the flip side of that are men who want their due benevolence but they refuse to protect and provide. They want their due benevolence but she's saying, "Ain't nothing going on but the rent." We both have responsibilities, don't we? Those responsibilities are delineated so that we are able to make sure the relationship is not taken advantage of. She has a supply, he has a supply and when they take care of each other by bringing the supply, then that's when you have a successful covenant. If she refuses to take care of him and he will not take care of her, then there's a problem regardless of who's right and who's wrong.

Most of the time, we are more concerned with pointing the finger across the table as opposed to recognizing that we are not bringing our supply. Many times, both people are being killed because once they feel they're not being supplied, they stop bringing their supply. Covenant is not predicated upon the other person bringing their supply. You are covenanting (promising) that you are going to bring your supply and if you don't, regardless of the person you're dealing with, then you are in breach of contract just as much as they are. Covenant was dissolved because of that reason.

They used to have what they would call The Covenant of Salt. Salt used to be more valuable than gold, so people would carry pouches of salt, and if they created a covenant with someone they would reach down in their salt pouch, grab a handful of it, and drop it in the other person's pouch. You couldn't go back in that pouch to pick out the grains of salt that the other person dropped

Covenant is not just a casual arrangement or agreement between two people. When you hear the term, "Cross my heart and hope to die," that is a covenant statement, even though it's most commonly spoken by kids. What we are saying is, "Cross my heart, and if I do you wrong…"

When you understand covenant, you recognize that it's more than just saying, "Hey, I got your back." You're saying their life is your life, and your life is theirs. You know the old statement, "His money is our money and my money is my money"? It does not work like that. When you cut covenant, what *we* have is what *we* have and *we* have equal access and equal rights to it.

Deuteronomy 8:18
"But thou shalt remember the Lord thy God: for it is he that giveth thee power to get wealth, that he may establish his covenant which he sware unto thy fathers, as it is this day."

"To establish" means to "achieve permanent acceptance of" or to show something to be true, certain and real. He said it is God who gives you the power. He enables you with the ability to prosper. I don't care what you think, God gave you your job. I don't care what you think has provided you the possessions that you have in your house, it was God. Whether you believe it to be so or not, it was God who gave you the power to be wealthy.

The reason why He gave it to you was to establish and to show you that His covenant with you is real, certain, for sure, all, and that He was going to honor His side of the covenant with you. Now the question becomes, when the topic of tithing comes up, why do you feel that it is not your responsibility to bring your supply to the other side of the covenant, to help establish, secure, show that you recognize covenant? Let me tell you a very quick story from 2 Samuel.

Jonathan and Saul are now dead. Mephibosheth is the next heir in line. The nurse decides to take Mephibosheth and run because she's afraid, as the next heir in line, that David's going to come and kill Mephibosheth. As she's running she drops him and permanently damages his leg. Now, years later, they happen to find out where Mephibosheth is and David says, "Go get him." The presumption would be that David is trying to remove any threat to his kingdom by removing the only heir that could oppose him. When David finally gets Mephibosheth in front of him, Mephibosheth is like, "Look, please let me just serve or something." David says, "No. Make sure he sits at my table. Make sure you dress him in the best. He can't walk for himself so I want you to go till his land for him. I need him to be taken care of." There's a reason why David did that; because he cut covenant with his father Jonathan and said, "What I have is what you have and what you have is what I have."

Running from a covenant with no understanding is what caused him to be crippled for the rest of his life. If you don't understand covenant, it will cripple you because you don't see what God's about to do in your life. God is not looking to punish, God is looking to reward. It was not based on the character of Mephibosheth, it was based on the character of David who cut covenant. David said, "Bring him in here, we're going to take care of him because I made a promise to his father." You might be hobbling along now spiritually, financially, or physically because you don't understand and then run from the very covenant that's meant to bless you.

He said, "I give you the power to get wealth so that I may prove and establish that my covenant is real." In other words He said the reason why He give you the power to prosper, the only reason why He give it to you, is so that He might be glorified, that His covenant may be seen in your life; that people may look at you and know that you serve the God of Abraham, Isaac and Jacob. If that's the case then if we are operating in lack, does that bring any glory to God? We're all at different places and we all struggle. I'm not making light of that. I'm trying to help you understand that it is God's desire to move you into a place of prosperity.

When we say that He will do exceedingly and abundantly more than you could ask or think, He said if your mind can conceive it, He can one-up it. If you can dream it up, He can still top it, exceedingly and abundantly more than you can ask or think. When we understand that He said He wants to establish His covenant, He's saying He wants to make it permanent. Covenant was always to generations and generations. If you made covenant with somebody, your children and your children's children are the benefit of the covenant. They can choose to reject it and they can walk away from it, but if they stay in it the covenant does not stop. If your children's children's child chooses to function and operate in covenant, they have equal access and rights to the covenant. If they decide not to then they don't receive a dime. That's why the Bible says that God keeps the covenant to a thousand generations.

Genesis 15:1
"After these things the word of the Lord came unto Abram in a vision, saying, Fear not, Abram: I am thy shield, and thy exceeding great reward."

This statement is a bit of a rarity in terms of Hebrew translation because very rarely will you find three words to explain English words. Most Hebrew words require a lot of English words to fully explain what it means. It's almost like the example of "cut covenant". "Cut covenant" is an idiom. It's like saying, "Jimmy

156

kicked the bucket." It requires context. If you walk up to somebody who does not know what that means they will literally think that Jimmy walked around and kicked a bucket, but what it implies is that Jimmy died. "Exceeding great reward" means the following: "Quickly increasing salary." When God was looking to come unto Abram He said, "Fear not I am your shield." He said, "Number one, I am your protector. I'll rebuke the devourer for your sake." In other words, He's saying He'll keep your enemy off of you. Then He says, "I am also your exceeding, great reward," which, again, means "quickly increasingly salary." He said, "I will be not only your protector but your quickly increasing salary."

Notice that the reason you would fear is because you have a lack of provision, protection, partnership and preservation. In some area where there would be lack, lack always brings about fear. If you want to see somebody become nervous, let them run out of money. It's a recognition of lack and now they're not sure if God is going to supply. If we want to be honest, it's a lack of faith.

God said to fear not because He is your quickly increasing salary. You think, "I can't get a job promotion." Yes you can. "Well they won't promote me," you say. Well, that might be a product of your personality because that does not mean that God will not promote you or move on your behalf.

The following example is very, very common situation so let's just say this person's name is Biff. Biff is getting involved in the ministry, growing spiritually and things start to change in his life. He then says, "God's blessed me with a job, but it requires me to work on Sunday." So, my response is, "Don't do it." Biff continues, "But you don't understand, I have bills to pay." I still say, "Don't do it. If you are going to consecrate to God His sabbath and His Sunday for worship to Him, then if He brought you the job it would be one that would honor Him. Why would He bring you something that would not honor Him?" So then Biff says, "Well you know, I have to do it. I'll just do it for a couple weeks."

Do you remember in the old movies when a women would become hysterical how the man would slap her? You'd think that was an act motivated by aggression, but it was not. It was a pattern interruption. It doesn't have to be a slap — it could be a glass of water to the face, or maybe a silly face or something — whatever it is that breaks the pattern right then and there is the goal (I am *not* telling you to slap anybody in the face!) because once you break the pattern, the behavior changes. So what Satan knows about you is that once you start coming and you start growing, what he's going to have to do to you is break the pattern because that's the issue of consistency.

What separates a Michael Jordan from Billy Jim Bob Smith (which nobody's heard of) is that he's consistent. Every time he shows up, he brings his game. So in order to break that game, inconsistency has to take place. Now, Biff was thinking he would just take the job for a couple of weeks, but now he's gone. You never see him again, his life takes on a whole new pattern and he moved away from the things of God. It never fails.

How many realtors do you know that are not ever working nights and weekends? That's unheard of, except for this one when I was in the business. I refused to work nights and weekends because I taught Bible college two nights a week, a Thursday night service and I had two services on Sundays, and I never missed a message my pastor preached. I made the commitment that if I understood the covenant that my God has with me, then my job on my side of the fence is to do what's right concerning Him. If I do that, then He becomes my quickly increasing salary. However, if I'm disrespectful in my relationship with God, then I will think that I'm in covenant with Him, but I'll really be in league with the devil and I'll go do what the devil wants me to do. I would establish my covenant and make it sure, true and real with him and not God.

I cannot tell you how many times I've preached it, I've said it, I've screamed it from the mountain tops. The realities are it's very hard for people to move past their flesh to arrive at that place. They'll say, "Wait a minute, I have to do something!" Yes, you have to do something, absolutely. God does not bless the seat of your pants, He blesses the work of your hands. However, the work of your hands should not impede upon praise and worship to Him. When He's telling Abram not to fear, He's courting him for the purposes of establishing a covenant with him.

Genesis 15:8-10

"And he said, Lord God, whereby shall I know that I shall inherit it? And he said unto him, Take me an heifer of three years old, and a she goat of three years old, and a ram of three years old, and a turtledove, and a young pigeon. And he took unto him all these, and divided them in the midst, and laid each piece one against another: but the birds divided he not."

Notice the necessity of the animal's age (three years old) and relate that to Jesus' ministry. What they would do while cutting a covenant was split the animals in half. The two people would stand back-to-back and then walk in a figure eight (the infinity symbol). They would end up back where they started, now facing each other, shake hands and say, "If I break this covenant, let be done to me what was just done to these animals." They would then walk through the midst of the blood as a sign of their covenant, and if they broke it they'd be cut in half like these animals. So when I told you the story earlier about King Xerxes cutting the man in half, you may think that was pretty gruesome and I agree, but the son broke covenant when he tried to go home and take care of his family.

It's funny how people will use their family to break covenant as if King Xerxes would have said, "Oh you have to go home and do what? I'm so sorry. Yeah, send dad and mom my life. Go ahead, go in peace." No, King Xerxes said, "Your covenant with me supersedes your relationship with them." This was something both parties understood, but it's amazing how people will violate God in the name of their family.

Genesis 15:12
"And when the sun was going down, a deep sleep fell upon Abram; and, lo, an horror of great darkness fell upon him."

Genesis 15:17
"And it came to pass, that, when the sun went down, and it was dark, behold a smoking furnace, and a burning lamp that passed between those pieces."

We understand that He promised Abram to be his quickly increasing salary. He is seeking covenant with Abram, Abram's demonstrating that he's going to accept it because he says, "How shall I know that I'm going to inherit all of this that you're telling me? How do I know you're going to give me the covenant you just said and honor it?" So He said, "Take these animals and split them apart." He's getting Abram ready to do a covenant ceremony and showing him how to know a covenant is about to be cut.

Now, my question is, as the smoking furnace moved between the pieces and God was getting Abram ready to cut covenant, who did God cut covenant with? It says a deep sleep fell on Abram, so if Abram was asleep and covenant was being cut Abram was not the one who cut covenant was he? How could you be a asleep and cutting covenant all at the same time? He said a smoking furnace passed between the pieces through the blood. Now, we understand that when Jesus' return is described, the Bible says His feet will be burnt like brass, His hair will be tight wool, and it says His voice would be like a thousand waters.

There was a fourth man in the furnace with Shadrach, Meshach and Abednego described as an image of fire, likened unto the son of God. So my question to you is, if we understand the smoking furnace, the son of God being likened unto a fire that is all-consuming but does not burn, then the question becomes who passed between the blood of the animals and cut covenant? It was Jesus. Most people think Jesus just showed up with the virgin Mary. That is not true, Jesus had a pre-incarnated ministry and He had an earthly ministry, just as He has a priestly ministry now because He is not dead.

Genesis 22:14

"And Abraham called the name of that place Jehovah-jireh: as it is said to this day, In the mount of the Lord it shall be seen. And the angel of the Lord called unto Abraham out of Heaven the second time, And said, By myself have I sworn, saith the Lord, for because thou hast done this thing, and hast not withheld thy son, thine only son."

He just showed his end of the covenant. God cut covenant and expected Abraham to sacrifice his only son and Abraham went up on mountain. He called it worship. Notice he wasn't running around the mountain chasing after his child. Even when the boy asked, "Who are we going to sacrifice?" Abraham responded with, "Just grab some wood." "But don't we need something to sacrifice?" "Boy, I said grab some wood!" "Okay I'm going to grab the wood. Got the wood. Okay, now, who are we sacrificing?" I'm like that kid. I'm not going anywhere until you explain to me being sacrificed. However, he said he took him up there, he was about to sacrifice him and the angel stopped him and said, "I know that now nothing you have is withheld from me. Now I know, but I have sworn by myself."

Hebrews 6:13

"For when God made promise to Abraham, because he could swear by no greater, he sware by himself,"

You know you're in control when you can say, "I'm going to cut a deal but ain't nobody else out here as good as I am so I'm going to cut the deal with myself." I want you to understand why He did that. Abram was a human who could make mistakes. If God cut covenant with Abram, the result would have been exactly the same as the covenant God had with Adam and Eve. Once it was broken then God would not have the ability to establish the covenant. A covenant could not be established if it was rooted in the frailties and inequities of man. God decided to cut covenant with Jesus, which is basically cutting it with himself, that way He knew it would never fail. That's why it says if you believe in Christ you are now Abraham's seed. Now you are heirs according to the promise. Not because you were great, not because you are smart, not because you earned it, but because the right and the privilege was transferred to you as a benefactor of what God promised to Abraham and Jesus ran it out.

So because he walked it out with zero faults, zero problems, zero issues, you now have access to a covenant that you were not a participant in but you are the recipient of. So I don't care if you messed up. I don't care if you made mistakes. You are not the one who's cut in half if you mess up. The one who's supposed to be split into pieces if he messed up was Christ. Which, notice, He was split into pieces for something that He didn't do in the event that you mess up. It's already done.

It has nothing to do with me. Why am I authorized to walk in prosperity? It was already bought and paid for. Even if I mess up, that was bought and paid for, too, because Christ has already paid the price on the cross for me to walk in it. If I reject it, I can do that. However, I will not—I could, but I will not. I understand that I have a covenant right, not of my own accord but because my God had enough sense to say, "I am not going to let them cut covenant with me again because they can't keep it... Because I could swear by none greater, I'm going to swear by myself that way I know that I will never break covenant with myself."

Verse 14 says, "Saying, Surely blessing I will bless thee, and multiplying I will multiply thee. And so, after he had patiently endured, he obtained the promise." If you mix up that relationship, you'll think that APS and IBM are your providers. Let me make sure you understand: **your source is *not* your employment. Your source is *not* your family and friends. Your source is the God** who said, "I'm going to cut covenant with you, but because I could swear by nobody greater than me I'm going to go down there and do it myself." Can you imagine the love He felt when He said, "I'm going to step off my throne and I'm going to come down here and walk through the blood that was shed by these animals, the blood of Christ that was shed for you, the spotless lamb. I'm going to bring the blood to a place of recognition for you to see that every time you see the blood of Christ you know I have covenant with you. Every time you see bloodshed you know I have covenant with you." It's the blood that is the life source of the body.

Now when you deal with God, if you know your God, you are not saying, "Um, hey you know if you're not busy or nothing, um could you, you know... I need some help?" The Bible says you come boldly before the throne of grace that you might obtain mercy. God said to put Him in remembrance. He hasn't forgotten,

He's trying to make sure you have not forgotten. When He says, "Put me in remembrance," He's saying, "Tell me why you want this." Your response should not be "Because I'm a good child." That's not good enough, but when you come boldly before the throne and say, "Because I'm a covenant child I have a right to this."

Jesus walked up to woman who was bowed up with infirmity for 18 years and said, "Woman thou art loosed from your infirmity." She was loosed from that moment. The Pharisees became angry and said, "Why are you doing this on the Lord's day? We aren't supposed to be out there working and you're violating that law." Jesus responded by saying, "This woman is a daughter of Abraham." That was the first response. Then He said, "You guys have donkeys and you will take your donkey and loose it to put water in your donkey but you don't think that this daughter of Abraham should be healed?" He was saying that the covenant had the right to heal her body, prosper her financially, and bring her healthy relationships. That covenant daughter of Abraham was a sign that she was a covenant woman. Since she was a covenant woman, sickness had no right to impede her body.

Lack has no right to take your finances; nothing should come against you because you are a covenant child of God and He keeps covenant to a thousand generations. It is not about your commitment or your character (you should have some because it should impel you to want to give to God, to want to support the work God has, to want to love God with everything you have). You should want to because of the covenant, but even if you do not, God said, "I got this because I didn't cut covenant with you, I cut it with myself." So even if you mess up, keep it moving.

ACCESSING
The Benefits of the Promise

The four P's of covenant are provision, protection, preservation, and partnership. We understand that provision resolves lack, protection brings safety, preservation continues and protects a heritage or a bloodline and partnership is established so that a relationship would not be taken advantage of. We know that God said He could swear by none greater so He swore by himself. So in this we can clearly see that you are the benefactor of a covenant but you are not a participant in the covenant. You're not the responsible parties for the covenant but you are the benefactors or the heirs of a covenant.

When people measure themselves to see if they fit the criteria for the covenant, they extract all the things they've done wrong in their life and they say, "Well I'm just not qualified." You're right, you're not qualified to walk out the covenant in terms of executing the covenant, but you *are* the recipient thereof. Whether or not you are the smartest person or dumb as a box of rocks, it does not matter; it does not change whether or not you are the recipient. Some people struggle with their own self image and they believe that God looks at them in the same way. That is not the case. God worked this thing out for you, because of you and in spite of you.

Deuteronomy 8:18
"But thou shalt remember the Lord thy God: for it is he that giveth thee power to get wealth, that he may establish his covenant which he sware unto thy fathers, as it is this day."

The word "establish" means to achieve permanent acceptance of or to show something to be true and certain. He gave you the ability to prosper so that you would, in fact, be able to know that His covenant with you is both true and certain that it's a fact and that He's showing it to be real.

We had an interesting question on our Facebook church page that asked if we preach a prosperity gospel. So, I responded as tactfully as I could but I wasn't quite sure what that question was trying to say because the opposite of a prospering gospel would then be a poverty gospel. I'm not familiar with that one either. I do not know what good news it would be for me to tell you you're going to be sick and poor, so I'm not quite sure what the question was about. So my response was, *"We preach the gospel, period. And in the gospel it contains things that refer to our prosperity but not to the excess of that we just believe money, money money. But we know that we are to prosper physically, financially, in our health and physical bodies so that He can establish His covenant."*

That's a sign that He is remaining true and certain to you. So when the question came about my first real response was going to be, "Is there any other type of gospel?" I'm unaware there's another gospel out there that does not tell us that God wants and expects us to be well, that He expects to be whole, abundantly supplied. I assume that his reference was to the extreme nature of where people have gone beyond the gospel and taken it into, "It's all about money." That type of thinking is very dangerous. You shouldn't reject God's desire to bless you. If you were to say that I'm blessed, it means that I'm empowered to obtain wealth or to prosper.

When you say, "I'm blessed," You're saying, "I'm empowered to prosper." For it is God that giveth you that power so in other words the blessing of the Lord is what maketh rich and adds no sorrow to it. What is the blessing? The blessing of the Lord is to help you and to enable you to prosper. So when he says that it is He that giveth you the power to gain wealth, then how do we ever extrapolate from that we are to be poor? He does this for one reason and one reason only and that's to establish His covenant, or to make His covenant certain, true and real. He does it to reveal himself in a way that you would know that God is here.

That's what establish means, to bring about a permanent acceptance of the reality of God's desire is to prosper you. I don't have to keep saying this but we're not talking about just money. There are people that have money longer than train smoke and so sick they'll never be able to spend it. I'm talking about whole prosperity, shalom. Shalom is a word that is often translated as peace. However the total definition of shalom is "whole" and if you're whole you'll have peace. It is, in part, meaning peace, but it means that you are whole, that you have everything you need. You are whole health-wise, whole in your relationships and in your finances.

When you truly have all that you need, there's just a certain peace that comes upon you where you're not anxious and you're not rushed because there's nothing that you need. The Bible says "wanting nothing" because you have all and you're abundantly supplied more than you can ask. Concerning covenant, you have to understand that God's saying, "If you will follow me, if you will love me, I will make my house your house. I will make my bank account your bank account, I will make my body your body so that whenever you need something, if you make your house my house, your life my life, then I cross my heart and hope to die."

Everything in God is being made ready for your disposal and of course everything you have is supposed to be made ready at His disposal. Unfortunately, that's usually where the struggle starts. We can rally around the idea that I have access to all that God has access to, but when God wants to have access to your life, your finances or your new car, it's somehow a problem. God tells you to give something and your response is, "Satan get thee behind me!" It's the saddest thing in the world. If you think about it, He's the one who did everything to make covenant with you and all He wanted from you was fellowship. His desire was to be in perfect fellowship with you in the way that He originally designed you to be prior to Adam and Eve's fall. All He's asking is to walk with you in the cool of the day, to spend time with you, and for a life traded for His. Yet and still when people apply that personal aspect to it, when it's hitting their pocketbook, their life and their time, "You know I'm busy. I got things to do, I don't have time." It's a sad place to be.

Genesis 22:17-18
"That in blessing I will bless thee, and in multiplying I will multiply thy seed as the stars of the Heaven, and as the sand which is upon the sea shore; and thy seed shall possess the gate of his enemies; And in thy seed shall all the nations of the earth be blessed; because thou hast obeyed my voice."

I would challenge someone to answer these questions: How many stars are there in the Heaven and how many grains of sand are on the beach? God said, "I will bless you, multiply you, and then I will bless your seed." He was talking to a man that had no children at all. He told him something that was contrary to what his natural experience was telling him. He did not have children, yet God promised him so many children that they will be numbered like the stars and like the grains of sand on the beach.

Can you imagine Abraham going back and telling Sarah, his wife, "Hey, God said we're going to have so many children like the stars!" She probably said, "Really? Coming from who? And from *where*?" We have to see the extremity of it, the craziness that would have to ensue and the thought process that would occur when God is saying, "I will bless you and I will multiply you and your seed will be like the stars, like the sands on the beach."

Matthew 16:17-19

"And Jesus answered and said unto him, Blessed art thou, Simon Barjona: for flesh and blood hath not revealed it unto thee, but my Father which is in Heaven. And I say also unto thee, That thou art Peter, and upon this rock I will build my church; and the gates of Hell shall not prevail against it. And I will give unto thee the keys of the kingdom of Heaven: and whatsoever thou shalt bind on earth shall be bound in Heaven: and whatsoever thou shalt loose on earth shall be loosed in Heaven."

Jesus is telling Simon that the gates of Hell shall not prevail against the church. Genesis says that Abraham was promised his seed shall possess the gates of his enemies. If I have possession of your gate, then I have access to it. I'm not going to pick up your gate and your wall and bring it home with me. There's a TV series called *The Tudors* on Netflix and it's about Henry the Eighth. When he took a particular city, they showed up and gave him keys to the city, which meant he could come and go as he wished and desired. Even if they lock the gate it does not matter how big the wall is.

If you have keys to the gate then you can have access, or entry. Abraham was promised that all of his children and his seed would possess the enemies gates and here we see where Jesus is telling Peter that the gates of Hell will not prevail against the church. He says, "behold I give you the keys." The key to the gate is this: whatever you permit will be permitted, and whatever you stop will be stopped. However, it will be up to you to make a choice in terms of whether or not you understand your inalienable rights. If you run around thinking that you have no abilities, then the gates of Hell will prevail against you because you don't have the key to the gate. The key to the gate is your recognition and understanding that you are a covenant child and that the gates of Hell will not prevail against you.

You are a covenant child and you have a heritage and a right that tells you that even when the enemy brings his attack, you hold the key to the gate to go through it. It does not matter how big of a fortress I build; if I install a door and I have the key to that door, I have access into the fortress. It could be 30ft wide, constructed of steel and concrete and made nuclear proof, but if I know how to go through the door, its design does not matter, does it? God's covenant has assured you that you will always possess the key to anything that the enemy wages against you, and that's what real covenant is about.

I hope you don't think God is afraid. He's not saying, "Hey, you know, that weapon I've never seen before..." God said, "I created the one who creates the weapons." He's not behind the weapon, but He created the one who creates the weapons. If you create the one who creates the thing, then you are not scared of either one because you created them. We have, unfortunately, a Frankenstein theory in terms of Satan and God. We think that the creation can eventually overthrow the creator, as did Frankenstein's creation. The moment that Satan tried to overthrow the creator Jesus said, "I beheld him fall from Heaven like lightning." In other words, it was a quick moment where his hind parts received the right foot of fellowship.

Can you imagine, just for a moment, sitting in on this scenario. Jesus is watching, the Holy Ghost is watching and God is sitting there on the throne. Everybody's relaxing and Satan comes in to talk about how he's in charge. God's just sends him down as fast as lightning, "*BOOM!*" You know how fast lightning moves? If you think in terms of the Frankenstein theory, that the creation eventually overtook his creator, then you'll have the wrong viewpoint of God. This is why when you wonder, "Well how come God doesn't remove Satan?" God's not afraid of him. There's nothing he can do to us when we're in Christ.

The only way he can attack you is when you are not in Christ and not acknowledging your responsibility and the provision and the protection that comes with your covenant. That's the only way he has access to you. Otherwise if we understand covenant, it tells me that if Satan attacks me, then he is attacking Him. Now, I may not have the ability to whoop Satan, but the one who created him does.

I remember when I was in early elementary school there was this huge 5th grader who, one day, was just harassing me to no end. He looked like a football linebacker; he must have flunked like six times. My brother's high school was right next door to my school, so he would pick me up after school every day and walk me home. I happened to tell him this kid was messing with me and bothering me. So my brother goes, "Lets go back." As we're walking back and he says to me, "If you see him you point him out." So I pointed him out. My brother walked up to the kid and said, "This guy right here, this is my younger brother. I go to school right next door, right here. If I ever catch you touching him again I'm going to punch you in the mouth." The little kid started popping off so my brother proceeded, too. As he picked himself up off the ground, he began to cry and he ran. So I never had a problem with him again. It is important for you to know that every time Satan attacks you, you have one that sticks closer than a brother to you. It's biblical, trust me. God will not allow you to be attacked when you're in Him because His covenant assures you protection.

Remember, He told Samuel, "Don't worry about these people," because Samuel was complaining that they were rejecting him. God said, "No, they're not rejecting you, they're rejecting me and they have a way bigger problem. They'd be better off if they were just rejecting you." Some of you wouldn't talk the way you talk if you knew God was right next to your school, your job, or your house. See, if you understood that you would have a certain degree of confidence. Being the little kid that I was, I was not scared of him at all after that. I walked passed him and looked at him like, "I dare you!" It changed my confidence level. I went from being scared, nervous, and jittery to now walking passed him going, "Boy I wish you would! By brother would be all over you like white on rice and a glass of milk on a paper plate in a snow storm." When you have that confidence, what do you have to be worried about? "Well, be careful. Satan might hear you." I hope he does hear me loud and hear me clear! He has no right to touch anything in my life— my finances or my physical body— because I'm in covenant with God Almighty, and whatever weapon Satan wages against me is waged against Him. I don't have to be the one to fight the battle because He promised me that He'd never leave me. However, if you don't know that, if you are not utterly convinced of that, how do you make it? The Bible says that the gates of Hell shall not prevail so if you feel like the gates of Hell are prevailing against you then you have to understand you have the keys. So, you either lock the door and tell him to stay on the other side of it, or you open the door and blindly let him come on in, but you are doing one or the other.

Numbers 23:16-20
"And the Lord met Balaam, and put a word in his mouth, and said, Go again unto Balak, and say thus. And when he came to him, behold, he stood by his burnt offering, and the princes

of Moab with him. And Balak said unto him, What hath the Lord spoken? And he took up his parable, and said, Rise up, Balak, and hear; hearken unto me, thou son of Zippor: God is not a man, that he should lie; neither the son of man, that he should repent: hath he said, and shall he not do it? or hath he spoken, and shall he not make it good? Behold, I have received commandment to bless: and he hath blessed; and I cannot reverse it."

Balaam was sent to wage an attack against the children of Israel. God sent an angel and the angel stopped right in front of Balaam while he's riding his donkey. Balaam couldn't see it, but the donkey could. So Balaam is now kicking and prodding the donkey to move but the donkey sees the angel standing there and will not move. So finally God allows the donkey to speak to Balaam. Now, I don't know about you, but that'd have been the last time I rode that donkey. "When is the last time I have not gone where you told me to go? Do you not see that angel sitting over there?" Could you imagine having that discussion? If a donkey can speak to Balaam and be used by God then I know that I have plenty of opportunity to be used by God. So Balaam is now speaking and he says, "God said that He is not a man that should lie and He's not like man that He should have to repent."

In other words, "God said to me to tell you that He's not a liar. Whatever He said, He meant, and He will not repent, which means whatever He said will happen. What He told me to tell you is that He's cannot reverse the blessing He gave to the people." Balaam said, "God told me to tell you the people you want me to attack, they're blessed and because they are blessed I cannot curse that which is blessed." God said, "I am not a man such as should lie and I'm never going to have to repent. If I said I'm going to bless those that bless you and curse those that curse you, if I say I'm going to bless you and multiply you, I will never have to eat my words. I will never have to repent. I will never lie to you so if I told you I'm going to bless you, if I told you I'm going to keep you, if I told you I'm going to prosper you so that I can establish my covenant then the very thing which I have proclaimed in your life will come to pass whether you believe it or not. It might not come to pass for you but I will not lie and you will not force me to repent."

Whatever God has blessed, Balaam said, "As much as you want me to curse those people I can't reverse their blessing." Nothing can reverse the blessing in your life. If you are blessed you cannot be cursed. Later on, Balaam says, "Look, why don't you just go on ahead and number me among them and curse me because I'm not doing this." Covenant is not something that is just to be taken lightly. When you understand it you can identify your relationship with God and realize that God is not some omnipotent, schizophrenic ruler who just sits on a throne and has not relationship with you. God said He wants covenant with you. The highest form of human covenant is marriage and God takes it one step higher.

Deuteronomy 7:9
"Know therefore that the Lord thy God, he is God, the faithful God, which keepeth covenant and mercy with them that love him and keep his commandments to a thousand generations."

He is always faithful and true and keeps covenant to a thousand generations. God will never break His word; God will never break His promise. He is faithful and He is true. You have a right to some things, but some people struggle. They think, "Well I have to ask God for it." There are some things that are inalienable rights. That's why David said to himself, "Forget not thy benefits." Certain jobs include benefits. If you have benefits or rights with by virtue of a covenant, whether or not you use your vacation hours, you still have the benefit of using them. Whether or not you use a 401k, profit sharing or any type of investment account that's offered, you still have access to them. The only difference is if you refuse to use them, you don't benefit from them. That's why David said, "Why are thou cast down O my soul? Forget not His benefits. Why are thou disquieted within me?"

In other words, "Mind, why are you so troubled? Soul, why are you so worried? Why are you in a place where you're struggling over whether or not you should be financially blessed and whether your finances are going to work or not; whether the relationships are going to work, whether your health and healing... why are you so disquieted mind? Why are you so unsettled? Why do you have such a lack of peace?" He had to remind his soul, his mind, will and emotions. He had to remind himself of his benefits. How many times do we have to remind ourselves of the benefits? Sometimes in your walk with God you just forget.

Now you're worried, you're afraid, you're concerned. You're like, "Oh my God, what am I going to do?" You're freaking out and the sky is falling and you just worry. People who worry, the Bible says, are like people without a God. Sometimes you have to remind yourself of your benefits package. "Wait a minute, I'm not going to be worried about this. This is part of my package. I have a right to this, I don't have to ask God to be healed, I am healed. I don't have to beg God to heal me, He already did it. I don't have to beg God to prosper me and worry Him to death with my prayers." The Bible says that he who was rich became poor. In case you have some biblical scholars out there that will tell you that was spiritually, that word used for "rich" refers to material, not spiritual. He who was rich became poor so that those who were poor might become rich.

Now, does being rich mean that everybody will be a billionaire? Of course not, but you should be abundantly supplied. You should have all of your needs met. You should not be ducking all the collectors and have an abundance of people trying to collect money from you. You should have an abundant supply unto everything that God has called you to. If you don't have that then it's time for you to study the word and develop a deeper understanding of your inalienable rights so you can stand up and profess and proclaim your rights as a believer.

These are not options. When you buy a car from a dealership you have a lot of options. You can buy the touring package and extra features as add-ons. Your base model, "Salvation" includes healing, prosperity, healthy relationships, and a healthy mind. When you first sign-up that's the benefit package you inherit. You might not have a lot of vacation, but I want you to understand it is a right.

So if you had a healthcare package and you needed to use that, you would go to the doctor. If they say, "We're not going to take your insurance." You'd say, "Somebody's going to take this insurance, I'm not going to pay for it myself because I have insurance." The company says, "Oh, we decided we're not going to give you insurance." Your response would be, "The devil is a liar. I took the job, you promised me insurance, where's my insurance?"

Why would you be so adamant about your insurance from a natural perspective, but yet you do not demand your spiritual benefits? You would make a scene and turn the doctor's office inside out, yet when Satan wages an attack against your body, the first thing you want to do is run to Walgreens and find some pills. You have a benefits package and it's the covenant that God has for you; He's given you access to a life in Him.

Galatians 3:7-9

"Know ye therefore that they which are of faith, the same are the children of Abraham. And the scripture, foreseeing that God would justify the heathen through faith, preached before the gospel unto Abraham, saying, In thee shall all nations be blessed. So then they which be of faith are blessed with faithful Abraham."

Verse 13 says, *"Christ hath redeemed us from the curse of the law, being made a curse for us: for it is written, Cursed is every one that hangeth on a tree: That the blessing of Abraham might come on the Gentiles through Jesus Christ; that we might receive the promise of the Spirit through faith."*

He's saying the Gospel, the Good News, was preached to Abraham before Jesus had ever shown up in the natural on His earthly ministry. When He said, "You shall have children as the stars of the sky and as the sand of the sea," He was talking then about you. Abraham did not have that many children naturally, but in the spirit he begat children that begat children, etc., so that the blessings of Abraham would come upon the gentiles by their belief in Christ who is the covenant maker. So the moment you confess Christ as your Lord and savior, you have been welcomed into the family of God. Now that you're in the family of God, the blessing of Abraham is now on you.

So, if the blessing of Abraham is now on you, then that which is blessed cannot be cursed. And, if you now have the same blessing that Abraham had, then you now understand that you have the right to protection, preservation, partnership, and provision in your life. It is not because of you, it is because of Jesus.

Jesus always was, but in the natural sense of the virgin Mary giving birth to a child, the gospel had already been preached. What's the good news? That all would be able to experience the blessing that was upon Abraham. How do you experience that? You confess Jesus as your Lord and savior and He now becomes your Lord and savior. Technically speaking, were you saved at the precise moment you confessed it? No, you were saved 2,000 years ago when He died on the cross for you. Whether or not it will reap in your life will depend on when you accept it. If a person never accepts Jesus, it's a wrap; they're not going to Heaven, even though they could have.

It's like a story that I've heard that sums this up very well. This is supposed to be true story, I don't know if it is or not but it's been told by a lot of different people, so you just assume at some point that it's either an old wive's tale or it's a true story. We'll just use it as if it were because the point is the same. The was a very wealthy lady that passed away and left her maid a painting that she just happened to adore all the time. This woman, the maid, hung the painting in her house (or apartment) and died poor. What was ultimately found out is that this particular painting was worth over a million dollars but the maid did not know it. Therefore she died having been poor, struggling, starving, cherishing and relishing in this painting, never having known that the painting was worth a million dollars. It's the same situation with people who don't recognize their covenant.

If you die without knowing Christ, you're going to Hell. It's that simple, but you don't have to because there's a valuable painting on the wall. You can struggle in your life with finances and health and all these things, but you don't have to because there's a painting on the wall. It's already been provided, you already have it, just ask for it. You have to make that confession. People say that what you don't know will hurt you. It is what you cause the reality is the Bible says my people perish for a lack of knowledge.

Why would you let somebody in your life go to Hell when Jesus died for them so they don't have to? What makes the difference and saves them from going to Hell is you telling them that Jesus died for them. You don't even have to do anything extravagant. It's not like we have to put them on the cross every single time; it's already handled. You don't have to go on the cross, all you need to do is report some information: "Let me tell you something you did not know. 2,000 years ago you were set free. You may not know it, but you were."

This is what covenant is all about and people struggle with covenant because they don't understand that on their wall they've got a million dollar painting. On their wall they have exactly what they need to resolve their problem. Here, we look at God and we're wondering, "God, how come you won't answer?" God responded with, "I don't know what they talking about."

Have you ever heard the joke about the guy who fell off the back of a boat? Nobody knew about it, but he's in the river drowning. Somebody walks by, sees him and says, "Hey let me throw you this branch and I'll pull you to shore." He's says, "No, I'm waiting for God to save me. He promised He would save me." So he continues floundering in the water, and another man in a boat comes by and says, "Hey, let me throw you this life raft and pull you in." Again, the man in the water says, "Nope, God's going to save me." Then a helicopter comes riding by and the pilot sees him in the water and says, "Hey, let's drop this ladder down and we'll pull you out." For a third time, the man in the water says, "No, God will save me." The man dies and as he's standing before God he's complaining. "You promised me you'd save me and you didn't keep your word!" God said, "I sent you a guy walking by, I you a boat and I sent you a helicopter. What else did you need?" Sometimes it's your perspective, your thinking and/or your pride that will cause you to drown.

I once had a dream 10-12 years ago where I had snakes wrapped around my arms and the heads were in my hands. I had no idea what this dream was, so I told my pastor about it and he said to me, "It's because you still believe that you can do everything. Those snakes wrapped around your hands are the ways and the things of the world that you're trying to use. Until you recognize that you can do nothing outside of God, nothing will ever work out."

You know how people always love rebuke? He was right, and from that moment forward I came to an understanding; that I'm always going to let God do what He wants to do. It may not be in my time, but He's always on time and if I don't trust in Him, I might as well forget it because my own doing can become my own undoing. You can create your own prison and not know you put yourself there. I can't tell you how many times people have said, "Well, Pastor, I'm on a fixed income." You know what I always say? "Who fixed it?"

You can put yourself, just by your thinking, in a box. Now all of a sudden, Satan keeps you at your limited level of revelation. He's not trying to allow you to grow up in Christ. He's not trying to let you believe just because your income is fixed in one area that God will bless you in another. It does not mean that you don't have a Picasso hanging on the wall or that you don't have an abundant supply somewhere. However, if you are so spiritually dull that you cannot be led by God, then you're never going to find it and you're going to be led by your senses and what you are capable of doing. What you are capable of doing is nothing compared to what God can do. However, you must believe Him, you have to trust Him and you need to know that He will do it all the time.

There's a place of peace that, when you're there, you just know you serve the God of more than enough. You serve El Shaddai, not El Cheapo, and if you serve the God of more than enough then He will abundantly supply your every need. Some people are stuck in jobs because they do not have a true revelation of what God can do for them. They have business ideas that God gave them and He's going to bless them. Make sure you're prayed up. Some of you are too lazy to run a business, but some of you do have a business idea that God's given you, yet you're afraid because you're stuck in a 9 to 5 mentality. It's Satan's wheel. He's not relegated you to a life of mediocrity.

The Bible says that the world should look at you and call you blessed. You know you're doing something when the world looks at you and sees how blessed you are. Look, people can look at you and call you blessed all day long church-wise. They can say, "You look blessed!" We throw those words around like they're nothing, but imagine how prosperous you need to be for a worldly person to turn around, look at you and say, "Wow! You are blessed!" That's what God wants to do in your life. Do you not understand that every mental picture you create, God one-ups? I do not care how you fashion it in your head, God still can do one better. He said He'll do exceedingly, abundantly more than you could ask or think. One of the biggest reasons people struggle financially is because they can't see the bigger picture. They think, "My family was poor, so as long as I own my own house I did better than them." Okay, how about buying somebody else a house? How about getting to the point where you have a whole compound that you're living on and you can be a blessing to somebody else? How about you can leave an inheritance to your children's children?

Do you realize that three of the top five richest people in America are Sam Walton's family? That man is dead and gone, but they're still some of the wealthiest people in America. A righteous man can leave an inheritance to his children's children. I'm trying to inspire you to a place where you dare to believe God because you are a covenant child. That woman who'd been bound for 18 years, she didn't have to be bound. She was a covenant child. When Jesus came and said, "Women thou art loosed," all He was telling her is, "You have a Picasso on the wall and it provides your healing. Why are you bowed up like this?" That's basically what He said.

Everything in your life that you are struggling and dealing with, you don't have to if you're a covenant child. Now, if you're not a believer in Christ then I feel for you. You get what you get, you get the crumbs. My blessing will leave some crumbs and you can have those, but if you are a believer in Christ you don't get crumbs, you get the full blessing and you get the exact same blessing that I get. We have to know we are covenant children because once you realize you're a covenant child, every time you walk passed the devil you have it in the back of your head, "My daddy will punch you in the mouth if you touch me again."

PRODUCING
Walking in the Covenant

It is Him that gives you the power to obtain wealth. Why does He do that? To give you the realness of Him and to establish in you the realness of His provision and the realness of His covenant. It's extremely critical we know that. I took a huge risk one Sunday by teaching on the subject of finances. Sometimes it's difficult for people to understand they're struggling financially because of how they treat God. In their minds, one has nothing to do with the other. But the reality is how you deal with God has an effect on what you receive from God. I don't know about you, but if you have children, I'm sure you love all your children, but you tend to give favor to the ones who treat you with respect. The ones that won't treat you honorably, I don't think you deal with them in the exact same way as you do the ones that treat you well. Just because they're your child does not mean they're a well-behaved child. Some of us have developed filters where we don't see their ill behavior and you think God does the same thing. The problem is God is not like you. When your child is acting out, you have the ability to ignore that, but our God is not so.

Genesis 14:18 - 15:1
"And Melchizedek king of Salem brought forth bread and wine: and he was the priest of the most high God. And he blessed him, and said, Blessed be Abram of the most high God, possessor of Heaven and earth: And blessed be the most high God, which hath delivered thine enemies into thy hand. And he gave him tithes of all. And the king of Sodom said unto Abram, Give me the persons, and take the goods to

*self. And Abram said to the king of Sodom, I have lift up mine
hand unto the Lord, the most high God, the possessor of
Heaven and earth, That I will not take from a thread even to
a shoelatchet, and that I will not take any thing that is thine,
lest thou shouldest say, I have made Abram rich: Save only
that which the young men have eaten, and the portion of the
men which went with me, Aner, Eshcol, and Mamre; let them
take their portion. After these things the word of the Lord
came unto Abram in a vision, saying, Fear not, Abram: I am
thy shield, and thy exceeding great reward."*

My question to you is when it says, "after these things" we
understand that Abram had already sworn unto God. When Abram
brought his tithe he brought it by faith. As He brought this by faith,
the Bible says after these things were done God then came to him
and said, "I am your quickly increasing salary. I am your abundant
supply." It came on the heels of Abram at the time because he
honored God. Through his honor, he gained the attention of God
because he did something before God did anything for him. It says
Abram brought his tithe.

Melchizedek said, "I don't want it you can have it, you
fought the battle and it's all yours." He said, "No, no. I've already
sworn by my hand that I would give this to God. When I do this, if
I don't do it then you'll have the right to claim you're the one who
made me rich." Now, obviously the amount that Abram gave was
enough to make somebody rich. Why, if God is no respecter of
persons, cut covenant for the benefit of Abram and regard Abram's
gift? If God is no respecter of persons, what was it about Abram
that put God in a place to do something with this guy? It's
covenant.

Genesis 15:1 AMP

"After these things, the word of the Lord came to Abram in a vision, saying, Fear not, Abram, I am your [a]Shield, your abundant compensation, and your reward shall be exceedingly great. And Abram said, Lord God, what can You give me, since I am going on [from this world] childless and he who shall be the owner and heir of my house is this [steward] Eliezer of Damascus?"

He's asking God, "What will you give me?" That would help you to understand that when he gave to God, in his mind he still has not received anything from God. He would say, "God I'm so grateful that I've received this million dollars that I've got to tithe off of. I'm so grateful that you blessed me with this first and I know you're looking after me and I know that you love me." He said, "What are you going to give me?" The implication is that he has yet to receive anything from God and he's wondering, "God what are you going to do for me?" His tithe was given by faith. God is no respecter of persons, but God is a respecter of faith.

Greater faith would be evidenced by greater behavior. So when you recognize covenant, you would then understand that it is not about what you think you should receive from God, it's about your responsibility to bring to God. There is not one person that I know who tithes that has to come to my church and asked for help financially. It's slightly interesting because one of the requirements that we have now eased up on is that a person does tithe before they come and ask the church for something. It's bizarre to me that you can ask for help from something that you don't ever contribute to. I know I'm making some enemies with this, but the truth is the truth.

Why is it that there are so many people that I know personally that since they've started tithing this is what they'll tell exactly like this, "I don't know how it all works out but it just seems to happen. My needs are met, my wants are provided for. I don't know that I make any more than I did before." How bizarre is it that we all will say the same thing? We know. Here's the tie-in. When you are acknowledging your covenant with God, you are honoring God with the first fruits of your increase.

There are things in your life that are not dealt with out of your bank account. If the very fabric of covenant is "What is yours is mine and what is mine is yours," then there are checks that are written that do not pull from your account. There are situations that are resolved, but not out of your account. There are occurrences that God sees and says, "Yeah let's go ahead and write a check for that," before you can even see, feel, taste, touch, or smell it from your natural perspective.

I don't know how anybody could live without having a supernatural bank account. If Satan's design is to constantly strip you naked of your health and finances, if that's his ultimate plan, then there has to be something beyond you to stave off that attack: His name is God and He created a covenant! Before Abram received anything, he puts his faith out before him and when God saw that He responded with, "Don't worry." Why tell Abram to not worry if he didn't worry?

Believe me, after you've written big checks you will always have that voice going, "You sure you're supposed to do that?" I can almost imagine Abram thinking to himself, "Do you know how much money I just tithed?" God responded with, "Fear not, I am your quickly increasing salary." In other words, what you gave will pale in comparison what He's about to do in your life. Then He said, "I am your shield (which means I'm your protector), I am your quickly increasing salary, I am your provider." Abram then said, "I don't have a son." The only thing that God didn't speak to was his lineage.

We understand the P's of covenant. There's partnership, right? He's already offering partnership by telling him, "This is what I'm going to do with you." Then He says, "I'm your shield, I am your quickly increasing supply." Which means He's going to bring provision to resolve any lack you ever have in your life. The only thing out of the four P's that God had not addressed is His lineage. He said, "I don't have any children." That's when God said, "I'm going to give you children that number the stars and the sand." God said, "This is what I'm going to do for you to establish my covenant with you."

Once you understand this, you will see that God will respond with the whole host of His angels and His bank account when you know you are in covenant with Him. How do you maintain your covenant relationship if you are unwilling to allow Him access to what you have? See we're proficient at commanding blessings to happen, "I command the blessing to come!" Really? Some can say that, even when God does not have access to anything you have or has limited access.

Psalms 109:28 AMP
"Let them curse, but do You bless. When adversaries arise, let them be put to shame, but let Your servant rejoice."

Psalms 109:26-29 MSG
"Help me, oh help me, God, my God, save me through your wonderful love; Then they'll know that your hand is in this, that you, God, have been at work. Let them curse all they want; you do the blessing Let them be jeered by the crowd when they stand up, followed by cheers for me, your

servant. Dress my accusers in clothes dirty with shame, discarded and humiliating old ragbag clothes."

He said, "Those that try to curse you cannot curse you because you are the last." He said, "Let them curse all they want, you do all the blessing. That which is blessed cannot be cursed." He says, "I'm the one that gives you the power to get wealth." The word "blessed" means "empowered to prosper." So when He says that He's the one that gives you the power to get wealth, He's telling you that He's the one who blesses you.

The reason why you are blessed is because you are a covenant child. As a covenant child you have a right to the blessing, and those who are blessed cannot be cursed. They acknowledge who they are as a covenant child. This is why in Malachi it says you are cursed with a curse because you're not honoring God. See, if you don't honor God you are not recognizing covenant.

If I'm in the middle of a battle and my family's in covenant with another family, I expect that family to come to my aid because we're in covenant. When I'm dealing with my enemy I'm not going to hold back because if I truly understand that I'm in covenant then what they have is actually mine. I will not act as if I have limited resources because I understand that I'm in covenant. So when I give, if I give knowing that I'm in covenant, I'm not doing it sparingly. I acknowledge that my bank account is not the only account that I have access to. So when people say they want to be blessed and they want to be financially this and that, it's funny because they give like poor people.

If you want to be financially blessed then you have to give like you are what you want to be. If you give sparingly, 2 Corinthians 9 tells us you will reap sparingly.

I cannot stand the rejection people have sometimes towards the Word of God. They're not rejecting me, they're rejecting the Word because there's no way you can refute proper doctrine. However, if you cannot receive or accept this then how will you be able to do anything else with God? What He's telling you is very simple. If you know you're in covenant then you deal with things differently.

If I have a million dollars in a bank account, you come to me and say, "I need five dollars," I don't have a problem with that. You might need one hundred dollars, and I still will not have a problem. You might need a thousand dollars and I won't have a problem. However, if all I have in my account is ten dollars and in my head that's all I have, if you come ask me for $10 you might get a fight because in my head that's all I have. If that's all I have (but yet honestly I'm in covenant with someone who has all the silver, all the gold...) then I'm going to constantly function below revelation because I'm always going to be looking at my bank account and not His. Once you understand it this way, it changes everything.

It changes how you view situations. Instead of always prying money out of your hands, if you have an unlimited bank account, you are not worried about it. Now listen, I'm not advocating being stupid! You're still a steward, you're responsible. You're responsible for the wealth and finances God gives you. Afterall, how can God bless you with more if you are not skillful with what you have? On top of that, if you refuse to acknowledge the covenant He cut with you and for you then how will you ever access it by faith?

Proverbs 10:22
"The blessing of the Lord, it maketh rich, and he addeth no sorrow with it."

I don't care what you do, it's the blessing that maketh rich. It's the blessing that empowers you, it's the blessing that will take care of you. The fact that you are in covenant with God gives you the right to say, "I am blessed. I'm empowered to prosper. Everything in the journey of my life, if I'm in covenant with God, has God's ability, His finances, His resources are at my disposal." Do they move when I want them to move? No, but if I'm in faith I have access to every single thing that God has.

Now you can acquire ten jobs if you want to and work until your fingers fall off, but I promise you, you will not prosper without God. This is what covenant is all about. It's about Him wanting your dependence to be on Him so that you don't breathe, you don't move, you don't think, and you don't act without His stamp of approval. Once you become dependent upon Him, now what you're saying is, "My life is your life and your life becomes my life." God will never take you out to dinner and skip out on the check. He'll never leave you, He'll never forsake you. You have to ask yourself, do you genuinely trust Him, and how much do you trust Him?

There's a balance to prosperity that must be understood. I think some have taken it to the extreme in one direction, but I also have a problem with people who took it to the other extreme saying that we're supposed to be poor. How will you be able to abound unto every good work if you're poor? How will you be able to take care of your family and your house? What testimony does it bring to God if you can't meet your obligations? What does that say to the world? You're a devout Christian, but you're as broke as can be. What does that do?

I saw somebody post this on Facebook, "If you don't like prosperity then you're going to hate Heaven." I responded with, "Great job, thanks for burning that sacred cow. Keep up the BBQ."

are bad and money is bad. Money is not the root of all evil, the love of money is the root of all evil. Money is a tool, it is good or evil by the hands that possess it.

If you don't believe me, take a football and put it in my hands. It's worth $20 in my hands, but put the same football in Michael Vick's hands or Brady's hands and it's worth $20,000,000. It's the same ball, the difference in value is based on whose hands it's in. I wish the body of Christ would wake up from this poverty mentality that is easy to believe. It's easy to believe for nothing because you'll have it every time. It's easy to believe for nothing, but why do we think we'll be able to make a difference in this world if we're just going to sit and complain about which president's in office, about what bankers are doing, and about what CEOs of major businesses are doing? If we're going to sit down and have that discussion then, in my opinion, the only discussion that is worth having is, "What are you doing to do about it? Because the only way you're going to put somebody in office that has ethics, character and morals is to raise one up."

The country has become so media-fied that instead of looking for character, all we want is *a* character. We become enamored with the show. How do you not think that it's God's desire to move finances into your hands so that you will do the right things with it? In Satan's hands it becomes destruction, but in the right hands it becomes prosperity and blessings to all.

Why is it so foreign to most people that if they would honor God then He will divinely move finances into your hands and give you God ideas that will cause you to invent something like the next internet, Twitter, Facebook or Amazon? Why is that not possible? Why is it so easy for us to believe that the world can prosper, but that God's people can only seem to bring their faith to the level of believing for nothing? (We knock that out of the park every single time!)

Is it so far-fetched to believe that God would want to prosper you because of your heart? If you don't tithe, I'm not talking to you right now. If you can't be trusted with what little God's already given you, I'm not talking to you. To those of you who *do* honor God in your finances, why is it so complicated to believe that God would want to bless you beyond measure? Why is it so complicated to believe God wants to give you businesses? Why is it so hard to believe He wants to give you vineyards you did not plant, houses you did not build? See, it's a measure of our faith. What can you believe Him for?

Genesis 24:34
"And he said, I am Abraham's servant. And the Lord hath blessed my master greatly; and he is become great: and he hath given him flocks, and herds, and silver, and gold, and menservants, and maidservants, and camels, and asses."
(That is material prosperity, is it not?)

Genesis 25:7-8
"And these are the days of the years of Abraham's life which he lived, an hundred threescore and fifteen years. Then Abraham gave up the ghost, and died in a good old age, an old man, and full of years; and was gathered to his people."

These two scriptures defined the end of Abraham's life. He said he was blessed financially, he lived to be a good old age, and he was surrounded by his family when he died. Health, prosperity, and healthy relationships are what God brought to Abraham's life. If the same covenant that Abraham functioned under is the same covenant that comes upon you by your faith in Christ, then you are able to believe God for your physical health, financial health, and for the health of the relationships around you.

Abraham died at a ripe and good old age; he didn't die early. He didn't die sick, he had health in his body. He had finances in his bank account and healthy relationships. If he had all those things, don't you know that you have a right to those things? There's a difference between saying that I have a privilege to something, versus having a right to something. I am not telling you what your privileges are, I'm telling you what your *rights* are.

Genesis 26:12
"Then Isaac sowed in that land, and received in the same year an hundredfold: and the Lord blessed him. And the man waxed great, and went forward, and grew until he became very great:"

Verse 1 says, *"And there was a famine in the land, beside the first famine that was in the days of Abraham. And Isaac went unto Abimelech king of the Philistines unto Gerar."*

There was a famine in the land, but Isaac still sowed in that land, not a new one. He did not say, "God, send me to a new place." He sowed in the same land where other people were experiencing famine, and he reaped a hundredfold. At the same time, when the world was going through a recession, depression, and oppression, one person (who was the child of a covenant man) understood covenant and said, "This is the same type of famine that affected my daddy, but my daddy still prospered." So he understood that and planted in the same time when everyone else is in famine, struggling, and having financial troubles. He sowed in the same land.

Can you imagine for a moment, he's planting in a field and it's growing like crazy, but the guy next door has dead vegetation because they're in famine? See, famine does not affect you because that which is blessed cannot be cursed. It says he sowed in that land at a time when the world was going through famine, struggling, and undersupplied. This is my point: Christians are in the world, being penalized by the world, for acting like the world and reaping what the world is getting. When all the while the Bible tells you that you are not of the world.

You are in the world, but you can be in it and not have what everybody else has. When everybody else is getting laid off, why do you think you have to be laid off? Why can you not be the only person left with a job? Our faith levels are not at that place. We are willing to believe for nothing and receive it. The verse is saying that Isaac sowed in that land and ticked off everybody else around him because he was prospering while they weren't. He understood he was a covenant child of God which meant whatever he put his hands to would prosper.

Whatever I put my hands to must prosper. Not "will" prosper, it *has* to prosper. Everything that I put my hands upon, if it's in my life, if it's under my staff, it has to succeed. This does not have a choice because I'm a covenant child of God. Even if I forget to water it, my God who can make rain fall from the sky will cause rain to fall upon it and water it for me.

The reason Isaac saw those results is because he was a covenant child. He did not need to find another place of business or a new land. He sowed in the same place as everybody else. You can see businesses failing, you can purchase the business for next to nothing and just because you're there, just because you physically have taken possession over it, it can turn all the way around. Just because it was famine for somebody else does not because it was famine for somebody else does not mean it's going to be famine for you.

If you are a covenant child, famine and recession do not affect you. If you are feeling the effects of it, you need to stop. Over the last three years as a church, our income — or however you want to say it — has gone up every single year by almost 20%. Whereas churches and some pastors I know are telling me, "I don't know what we're going to do now. We've got to shut this down, close that, we've got to shrink this, we got to fire that…" These are all things they're doing because the economy is affecting the church.

We have not had that problem because we're covenant children, but if the world goes upside down and we go with it, what are we serving? If our lives go upside down because of the world, who are we serving? Satan is not my master, God is my supply and everything I need shall come to pass. All the things that I will need in my life, God will supply according to His riches in Christ Jesus.

I believe that it's God's desire for me to prosper and be in good health even as my soul prospers. I am totally convinced that every need I have, if I honor God with the first fruits of my income, will be met and He will cause my barn to burst. I'll have everything I need, abundantly, if I honor Him first. Why wouldn't I? He knows I'm going to do what He wants me to do with it. There are other things I could have done, probably making three times as much money, but I spent what I didn't have, to do what nobody could see, to have what I knew God wanted. He supplied for it every step of the way.

You have to raise your revelation of covenant, of God, and who He is. Stop letting people tell you, "I tried that and it didn't certain that you are in covenant with Him. You can walk without covenant, and the sad part is that a majority of our Christian brothers and sisters live below the revelation line of covenant. They do not know what is God's is actually theirs. They are constantly approaching God asking, "Can I have it?" while God is saying, "I already gave it."

If you bought a house from me, I would give you the keys. If you call me two weeks later and say, "Could you let me into the house?" I'm going to hang up on you because I already gave you the keys. Don't call me about it. If you already have it and it's already been done, then what are you waiting on?